SALT

AND THE ALCHEMICAL SOUL

ERNEST JONES

C.G. JUNG

JAMES HILLMAN

edited with an introduction
by STANTON MARLAN

SPRING PUBLICATIONS
THOMPSON, CONN.

Published by Spring Publications
Thompson, Conn.
www.springpublications.com

Second, revised edition 2023 (2.0)

First published in 1995

The cover image of a "cosmic furnace," an alchemical apparatus designed
to unify sulphur, salt, and mercury, is taken from *Le vray et méthodique cours
de la physique résolutive, vulgairement dite chymie* by Annibal Barlet (Paris, 1653).

ISBN: 978-0-88214-131-2

Library of Congress Control Number: 2023933275

CONTENTS

Editor's Preface and Acknowledgments   5

STANTON MARLAN
Introduction   9

ERNEST JONES
The Symbolic Significance of Salt in Folklore and Superstition   37

C. G. JUNG
Sal   87

JAMES HILLMAN
The Suffering of Salt   127

Abbreviations

CW = *Collected Works of C. G. Jung,* edited and translated by Gerhard Adler and R.F.C. Hull, 20 vols. (Princeton, N.J.: Princeton University Press, 1953–79), cited by paragraph number

HM = *The Hermetic Museum,* translated by Arthur Edward Waite, 2 vols. (London: James Elliott, 1893)

MDR=C.G. Jung, *Memories, Dreams, Reflections,* recorded and edited by Aniela Jaffé, translated by Richard and Clara Winston (New York: Vintage Books, 1989).

Paracelsus = *The Hermetic and Alchemical Writings of Aureolus Philippus Theophrastus Bombast of Hohenheim, Called Paracelsus the Great,* translated and edited by Arthur Edward Waite, 2 vols. (London: James Eliott, 1894).

PL = *Patrologia Latina,* edited by Jacques-Paul Migne, 217 vols. (Paris: Imprimerie Catholique, 1841–55)

PG = *Patrologia Graeca,* edited by Jacques-Paul Migne, 161 vols. (Paris: Imprimerie Catholique, 1857–66)

SE = *The Standard Edition of the Complete Psychological Works of Sigmund Freud,* edited by James Strachey, 24 vols. (London: The Hogarth Press and the Institute of Psycho-Analysis, 1953–74)

UE = *Uniform Edition of the Writings of James Hillman,* edited by Klaus Ottmann, 12 vols. (Putnam and Thompson, Conn.: Spring Publications, 2004–)

Editor's Preface and Acknowledgments

The inspiration for this book emerged while reading an essay by James Hillman entitled "Salt: A Chapter in Alchemical Psychology."[1] In it, Hillman cited two major essays indispensable to alchemical psychology: Ernest Jones's paper "The Symbolic Significance of Salt in Folklore and Superstition," first published in *Imago* in 1912, and C. G. Jung's "Sal," a section of his *Mysterium Coniunctionis* (*CW* 14), first published in 1955. These three essays, collected here for the first time, form a cohesive background for reflection on the image of salt, the alchemical soul, and psychology. My goal is to provide an opportunity to reflect on the image of salt as well as on differing genres of depth psychology, the psychology of alchemy, and the emergence of an alchemical psychology.

While a historical curing and maturing is implied, the intent of this book is not aimed at a developmental judgment. While seasoning implies ripening, it is also the recognition and appreciation of flavoring, each approach yielding a certain relish, taste, zest, and interest to the matter at hand. Each essay tinges the material, and the material taints the approach: "The stuff of which we write becomes the stuff with which we write."[2]

I am deeply grateful to James Hillman. As a former analyst and mentor, and now as colleague and friend, he continues to stimulate my imagination. His passion and originality are inspiring, and to my mind, his work on the alchemical soul represents a new start, style, and genre of psychology.

---

1. "Salt: A Chapter in Alchemical Psychology" appeared first in the publication of papers of the Dragonflies conference in Dallas in February 1979 and was subsequently published in *Images of the Untouched: Virginity in Psyche, Myth, and Community,* edited by Joanne Stroud and Gail Thomas (Dallas: Spring Publications, 1982). It was revised by Hillman in 2010 and republished as "The Suffering of Salt" in *UE*5: *Alchemical Psychology.*

2. Hillman, "The Suffering of Salt," 71.

I also feel a profound personal appreciation towards Edward Edinger. Many years ago, as an analysand and analytic candidate at the C. G. Jung Institute of New York, I attended his Thursday night lectures on alchemy. His scholarly work exemplified a deep engagement in the alchemical process, and his respect for Jung and the psyche was infectious.

I would also like to thank Charles H. Taylor Jr., a Jungian colleague from New York, for his correspondence and permission to quote from the non-clinical chapters of his 1979 thesis, "Salt in Dreams and Psychotherapy: Images of Differentiation," an excellent work that merits separate publication.

Thanks is also due to Jay Livernois, who was managing editor at Spring Publications during the time of this book's original publication, for his enthusiasm, know-how, advice, and support.

I am grateful to Michael Flanagin, curator of The Archive for Research in Archetypal Symbolism (ARAS) at the C. G. Jung Institute of San Francisco. To him I owe the discovery of a number of the graphic images reproduced here. His interest and skill turned up results where others could find nothing.

I would like also to extend my thanks to the C. G. Jung Institute Analyst Training Program of Pittsburgh, the Inter-Regional Society of Jungian Analysts, and the C. G. Jung Educational Center of Pittsburgh for sponsoring my teaching and courses in Alchemy, which provided background support for this book.

I would also like to acknowledge and thank Terry Pulver, Lacanian psychologist and colleague, for his friendship and challenging intellectual stimulation. Thanks also to John Schulman, poet, teacher, friend, and owner of Caliban Book Store, for his astute reading, stylistic suggestions, and intelligent interest in this project. And thanks to my friend and colleague, Dr. Paul Kugler, for his careful and thoughtful reading of the introduction.

My acknowledgments would not be complete without mentioning some family members who have directly and indirectly contributed to this book. Special thanks to my father, Jack Marian, to whom I owe my first copy of *The Hermetic Museum* at a time when it was nearly impossible to get. To him and my mother, Sylvia Marian, I owe a lifetime of love, support, and personal consideration. Thanks also to my brother, David, for his faithfulness and friendship, and my uncle, Milton, who has over the years been like an older brother and given guidance in innumerable ways. Special thanks also to my wife, Jan DeVeber Marian, lover, friend, and intellectual companion, who has been a constant support and my best critic. I would like to acknowledge my daughters, Dawn and Tori, for their love and support and for their uncompromising intellectual and political integrity. Special thanks go to Tori for her help in reading the manuscript and offering her fine editorial skills in support of the project. And finally, thanks to my son Brandon whose sensitivity and indomitable spirit continues to inspire and amaze me. They have all salted my life and enhanced its pleasure.

It is with appreciation to Margot McLean and Klaus Ottmann that this newly revised 2023 edition of *Salt and the Alchemical Soul* is being published. Thanks to Dr. Ottmann for his careful editing, corrections, and aligning the text with James Hillman's *Uniform Edition*, giving the book a new zest.

🜔

In addition to Dr. Stanton Marlan's acknowledgments, the publisher is grateful for permission to reproduce the following material: Hogarth Press for permission to reprint Ernest Jones's essay, taken from *Essays in Applied Psychoanalysis*, 1951; Princeton University Press for permission to reprint an excerpt from Jung's *Mysterium Coniunctionis*.

STANTON MARLAN

Introduction

T his is a book about the imagination and images. Particularly, it is about the image of salt as an essential principle of the alchemical soul. We will follow salt as it draws forth ideas and essences from the history of human expression and discover a ubiquitous and mysterious substance that has been pursued down through the ages and across cultures. Throughout this book, salt is revealed as a carrier of excessive significance in the notion of the male fertilizing power (Jones), through the erotics of lunar symbolism (Jung), to the activation of the image as a psychological substance initiatory of an alchemical mode of psychology (Hillman).

Reprinted here are three of the most enthusiastic and imaginative essays from the margins of psychoanalysis and analytical and archetypal psychology in newly edited form. These papers reflect fundamental approaches to depth psychology, and each reflect a way of seeing both the substance and psyche of salt. Salt seems to have become not only a subject but the seasoning of depth psychology *par excellence,* and each way it is imagined, in Freudian, Jungian, and archetypal psychology, has its own unique flavor. Each essay invites reflection not only on salt but on a genre of depth psychology. The way an image is understood, developed, and deepened depends on the approach, on the style of the imaginal reality that reflects it. Through each approach a particular understanding emerges. Through each lens we are invited to read a development of analytic perspective: psychoanalysis applied (Jones), expanded (Jung), and brought alive (Hillman).

There are reasons why these writers consider the image of salt so important. Homer called salt a divine substance, and Plato described it "as especially dear to the gods." It has played a significant role in religious, ceremonial, and magical practices, from baptism to a charm against the devil. It has played a role in medieval Christianity in the Latin Church as *sal sapientiae* and in mystical writings and alchemy in the images of heavenly Sophia as sodium. The history of salt has "cast light in unexpected directions, as on the medieval foundations of monasteries, the causes of the French revolution, and on the environmental crisis of thr 20th century."[1]

The ceremonial use of salt has touched a wide range of human behavior, feeling, and expression, from marriage rites and customs to economics, from fertility to friendship, from superstition to the fundamental stuff of human life. Not surprisingly, salt has become a focus for depth psychologists. "Freud has shown that a by-way in psychology may lead to a country that yields an unexpectedly rich harvest," wrote Ernest Jones, and Jung has extracted a revolutionary psychology from the most arcane of subjects. One of salt's compelling metaphoric features is its continued appearance in various cultures across time and distance. To rewrite Blake, we can see the world in a grain of salt.

Fig. 1 The overturned salt cellar by Judas's right wrist is an omen of bad luck in Leonardo da Vinci's painting of the last supper.

1. Robert P. Multhauf, *Neptune's Gift: A History of Common Salt* (Baltimore and London: The Johns Hopkins University Press, 1978), xiii.

I. *Logos and the Patriarchy: Semination*

Ernest Jones, full of youthful enthusiasm and filial devotion to Freud, desired to contribute to Freud's developing science and extend its application towards an understanding of the psychological roots of superstition. Armed with the metaphors and methods of natural science and associationism, he set out to apply the light of psychoanalysis to the darkness of superstition, particularly the superstitions surrounding salt. Scientific method provides the infrastructure of Jones' essay, and absorbed in the conflict between science and supernaturalism,[2] he follows the rational architecture of inductive methods, hypotheses, and inferences from "definitely ascertained facts and then...test[ing] them in their capacity to resume the whole range of accessible evidence." Jones attempts to prove the value of psychoanalysis as a scientific procedure so that he may use its heuristic power to cut below the external point of view and discover what salt has essentially stood for in the human mind.[3]

No superficial investigation explains what Jones defines as the "excessive significance"[4] given to the superstitions of salt. Jones realizes that salt begins as a fundamental datum of reality, as part of the external world res extensa with an objective meaning inherent in its properties as a literal object. It is thus deprived of a fundamental, metaphoric nature.

2. *The Complete Correspondence of Sigmund Freud and Ernest Jones, 1908–1939*, edited by R. Andrew Paskauskas (Cambridge, Mass.: Harvard University Press, 1993), 115. From a letter dated 31 August 1911.

3. Jones's scientific orientation preceded his psychoanalytic work. In 1909 he published eighteen scientific articles in the field of neurology. In an early exchange of letters with Freud he suggested that Pearson's *Grammar of Science* "is the grandest exposition of the fundamental principles of science" and that as a student it inspired him "with clear and high scientific ideals." See *The Complete Correspondence of Sigmund Freud and Ernest Jones*, 49. Letter dated 30 March 1910.

4. From the very beginning psychoanalysis was concerned with explaining the nature and function of "excessively intense ideas." This phrase is found in the inaugural paragraphs of Freud's 1895 manuscript, "Project for a Scientific Psychology," in *SE* 5: 295. The above is noted by Richard Boothby, "'Now You See It...': The Dynamics of Presence and Absence in Psychoanalysis," in *From Phenomenology to Thought, Errancy, and Desire: Essays in Honor of William J. Richardson, S.J.*, edited by Babette E. Babich (Dordrecht: Springer Science+ Business Media, 1995).

Soul is separated from the world,[5] and so salt's excessive significance must be derived from an external source, from a more primary idea in the unconscious. For Jones this more fundamental idea is "overcharged with psychical significance," and the secondary idea may be said to represent or symbolize the primary one.[6] He arrives at this more primary idea by summing up his observations about salt:

---

5. Jones's scientific approach here can be contrasted with Hillman's, which begins: "Alchemical salt, like any other alchemical substance, is a metaphoric or 'philosophical' salt. We are warned in various alchemical texts not to assume that this mineral is 'common' salt" (127).

6. Ibid. Jones elaborates his notion of symbolism in his now classic paper, "The Theory of Symbolism," which was published in 1916, four years after he published his paper on salt. His work on symbolism is considered by some to be the most remarkable work of the Freudian School. An evaluation and explication of this work is summarized and critiqued in an important lengthy footnote in Paul Ricoeur's *Freud and Philosophy*, translated by Denis Savage (New Haven and London: Yale University Press, 1970), 502–5. In this note Ricoeur shows how Jones places symbolism in the general class of indirect representations. The symbols represent hidden or secret ideas. True symbolism, says Jones, 1) represents repressed unconscious themes; 2) has a constant meaning or very limited scope for variation in meaning; 3) betrays the limited and uniform character of the primordial interests of mankind-not in the sense of Jungian archetypes, but more as stereotypes; 4) is archaic; 5) has linguistic connections, strikingly revealed by etymology; 6) has parallels in the fields of myth, folklore, poetry. Thus, the range of symbolism is restricted to substitute figures that arise from compromise between the unconscious and censorship. All symbols represent themes relating to the bodily self and sexuality is a recurrent theme.

Jones claims this view of symbolism is scientific and critiques other approaches to symbolism. Ricoeur's critique here is relevant to the legitimization of other perspectives. He states, "Psychoanalysis has no way of proving that repressed impulses are the only sources of what can be symbolized. Thus, the view that in Eastern religions the phallus becomes the symbol of a creative power can not be dismissed for psychoanalytic reasons, but for philosophical reasons which must be debated on other grounds."

Ricoeur points out that Jones is disdainful of the view that symbols may have an "anagogic" meaning (Silberer), a "programmatic meaning" (Adler), or a "prospective meaning" (Jung). According to Jones these authors abandon the methods and canons of science, particularly the conceptions of causality and determinism. Again for Ricoeur the argument is not psychoanalytic but philosophical. For Ricoeur, such a position does not account for the eager symbolic domain in western tradition since Plato and Origin but only for the pale metaphors of ordinary language and its rhetoric.

> Salt is a pure, white, immaculate, and incorruptible substance, apparently irreducible into any further constituent elements, and indispensable to living beings. It has correspondingly been regarded as the essence of things in general, the quintessence of life, and the very soul of the body. It has been invested with the highest general significance—far more than that of any other article of diet...The durability of salt, and its immunity against decay, made it an emblem of immortality. It was believed to have an importance in favoring fertility and fecundity, and in preventing barrenness.

Having described the popular conception of the qualities he discovered, he goes on to say:

> If the word salt had not been mentioned in the preceding description anyone accustomed to hidden symbolism, and many without the experience, would regard it a circumlocutory and rather grandiloquent account of a still more familiar idea—that of human semen.

Semen then lends itself well to such associations and for Jones the idea of salt had acquired much of its significance from its being "unconsciously associated with that of semen." This "fulfills at least one postulate of all symbolic thinking—namely that the idea from which the excessive significance is derived is more important psychically than the idea to which this is transferred."

Thus far, Jones views his findings as a hypothesis that must now be proven by the "ordinary rules of science," and he uses anthropological material and folklore to confirm his hypothesis. Jones carefully enumerates his evidence, including mice becoming impregnated through eating salt and wedding customs in the Pyrenees, in which salt is put in the left pocket to guard against the man becoming impotent. He moves easily from Shakespeare to Frobenius, where he finds salt is a direct equivalent of semen.

The demands of scientific demonstration then press him to turn his attention to ontogenetically deeper roots, where he finds the idea of urine as an infantile equivalent to semen. Jones demonstrates that many of the customs and ideas he found associated with salt are duplicated with urine, including magical powers, healing and initiation ceremonies, and significant analogies to religious performances. One striking example is in regard to baptismal symbolism:

> All the evidence, from comparative religions, from history, anthro-
> pology, and folklore, converges to the *conclusion, not only that Chris-*
> *tian and other rites of baptism symbolize the bestowment of a vital fluid*
> *(semen or urine) on the initiate, but that the holy water there used is a lineal*
> *descendent of urine, the use of which it gradually displaced.*

Following his "scientific method" and understanding of symbolism,
Jones concludes that "the ideas of…urine and semen are interchangeable equivalents in the unconscious."[7]

Questioning whether or not natural scientific methodology is or
should be a criteria of psychoanalytic findings, Charles Taylor composed
a thesis offering an interesting critique of Jones, employing Jones's rules.
While appreciating the formidable extent of Jones's scholarship, Taylor
suggests he fails to live up to scientific method and follows a characteristically Freudian approach to the significance of an archetypal image.[8]

---

7. It is of interest to find validation for Jones's equation in Jung's early study of "a
case of neurosis in a child" in *CW*4: *Freud and Psychoanalysis.* In the tenth interview
with the child, Jung describes infantile theories about fertilization and birth: "The
child had always thought that the urine of a man went into the body of a woman, and
that from this the embryo would grow. Hence the child was in the water, i.e., urine,
from the beginning. Another version was that when the urine was drunk with the doc-
tor's syrup, the child grew in the head" (par. 512).

Compare this with Jung's later understanding in *CW*12: *Psychology and Alchemy* (par.
338, fig. 121). The figure depicts "the transformation of Mercurius in the Hermetic
vessel. The homunculus shown as a 'pissing manikin' is an allusion to the *urina puerorum* (=*aqua permanens*)" from the *Cabala Mineralis* (par. 338). Also side by side with
the idea of the *prima materia,* "that of water (*aqua permanens*)…play[s] an important
part…Like the *prima materia* the water has a thousand names; it is even said to be the
original material of the stone" (par. 336).

And in Hillman, "among the sources of salt, urine holds a special place. According
to the model of the macrocosm/microcosm, urine is the human brine. It is the microscopic sea within or the 'waters below'…Urinary salts are residual traces afloat in the
lower person…there is psychic life in the lower person independent of what goes on
above, and this life is an *intense, burning, personal necessity which no one else can tend for
you and for which time and place and privacy must be found*" (italics mine). Here one can
see Hillman's emphasis in bringing the image into a psychologically near experiential
understanding.

8. Charles H. Taylor, Jr., *Salt in Dreams and Psychotherapy: Images of Differentiations,*
(unpublished thesis presented to the C. G. Jung Training Center of New York, 1979), 5.

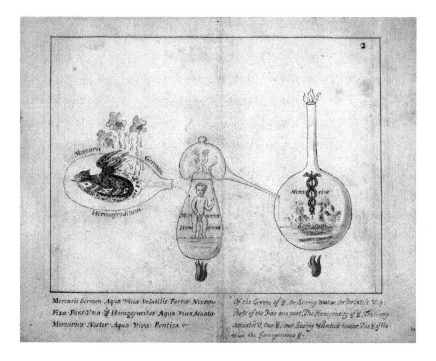

Fig. 2 CABALA MINERALIS, c. 1700. An illustration from the alchemical text *Cabala Mineralis*. Manuscript page by Rabbi Simon Ben Cantara, c. 1700. British Library/Granger, NYC.

It is a tendency of early Freudian interpretation "to pick out some partial congruence an image has with what it is said to represent"[9] and not to take seriously "those associations which deny his hypothesis."[10] Taylor points to the painful and darker associations absent in Jones's essay, such

---

Taylor's thesis adds to the psychoanalytic understanding of the image of salt as well as contributing to the methodology for studying it. His study is aimed at both an exposition of the symbolic meaning of salt, and to my knowledge is the only study based primarily on clinical cases. Beyond his critique of Freudian methodology in Jones and his support and critique of Jung, he offers a creative insight into what makes salt life supporting or life denying which he suggests has to do with the quantity. Thus for Taylor, salt is an important image of differentiation. His study also integrates modern studies on the physiology of taste as an empirically based starting point for an examination of salt in a way which attempts to stay close to its natural properties.

9. Ibid. 7.
10. Ibid., 12.

as "bitterness, the marah of the sea, its sting in wounds, the saltiness of tears, or its sterilizing power."[11]

Following a Jungian approach, Taylor analyses the way the many associations to salt link it to different qualities depending on the context in which it appears and chastises Jones for lumping them all together, "forcing all interpretation into a pre-determined conclusion."[12] For Taylor, like for Jung, salt is more feminine than masculine,[13] and it is the "patriarchal bias" of the early Freudians which forced all interpretation into a single mode and influenced Jones's "selection of semen as the hidden reference behind the...association to salt."[14]

It is ironic that Jones was suppressing feminine, sea-related imagery of salt. He subjected himself to Freud in much the same way he subjected the image of salt to a patriarchal bias. Freud praised Jones for his willingness to subordinate his personal ambition to "the interests of the cause,"[15] and Jones replied "therefore my work will be to try to work out in detail and to find new demonstrations for the truth of ideas that others have suggested. To me, work is like a woman bearing a child; to men like you, I suppose it is more like the male fertilization."[16] The semen that Jones unconsciously discovers might be said to be Freud's, the seed that originally inseminated him. Semen then has an excess, a more polyvalent potential that may include Jones's observations, but in the end exceeds his reductive attempt to master the image.

While semen has a definite sexual connotation, it also possesses many other meanings. For Jung,

> Freud's idea of sexuality is incredibly elastic and so vague that it can be made to include almost anything. The word sounds familiar enough, but what it denotes is no more than an indeterminable X that ranges from the physiological activity of the glands at one extreme to the sublime reaches of the spirit at the other. Instead of yielding to the dogmatic conviction based on the illusion that we know

11. Ibid., 3.

12. Ibid., 12.

13. Ibid.

14. Ibid., 7.

15. *The Complete Correspondence of Sigmund Freud and Ernest Jones,* 59. Letter dated 22 May 1910.

16. Ibid., 61. Letter dated 19 June 1910.

something because we have a familiar word for it, [e.g., semen], I prefer to regard the symbol as an unknown quantity, hard to recognize and, in the last resort, never quite determinable.[17]

Jones's one-to-one pairing of salt and semen ignored the breadth of covert and archetypal associations that a powerful emblem like semen contains. If Jones in the name of science tried to be ambiguous, Jung in the name of empiricism capitalized on ambiguity.

Jung's comments throw light on the use Jones makes of Paracelsus's *De Origine Morborum Invisibilium* to substantiate his own thesis and demonstrate the connection between salt and semen. Paracelsus teaches, "Incubi and Succubi emanate from the sperma found in the imagination of those who commit the unnatural sin of onan, but that this is no true sperma, only corrupted salt." Jones uses this example to deftly link the idea of salt with that of semen.

However, to Paracelsus, like Jung, the image of sperma is much more complex and filled with ambiguity. Franz Hartmann, in his book on the life and teachings of Paracelsus, cites him saying:

> Imagination is the cause of Incubi and Succubi and fluid Larvae … This sperma, coming from the imagination, is born in *Amor Hereos*. This means a kind of love in which a man may imagine a woman, or a woman a man, to perform the connubial act with the image created in the sphere of mind. From this act results the expulsion of an ethereal fluid, impotent to generate a child but capable of bringing Larvae into existence.[18]

Commenting on the meaning of sperma, Paracelsus notes the distinction from its common meaning. He states: "This semen, however, is not the sperma of the visible seminal fluid of man, but rather a semi-material principle contained in the sperma, or the *aura seminalis,* to which the sperma serves as a vehicle,"[19] and further: "the physical sperma is a secretion of the physical organs, but the *aura seminalis* is a product (or emanation) of the *liquor vitae.*"[20]

---

17. "The Practical Use of Dream Analysis," in *CW* 12, par. 340.

18. Franz Hartmann, *The Life of Philippus Theophrastus Bombast of Hohenheim Known by the Name of Paracelsus and the Substance of His Teachings* (London: Kegan Paul, Trench, Trübner, & Co., 1896), 109–10.

19. Ibid., 72.

20. Ibid. The *liquor vitae* is *Prana,* a nerve fluid, in which, according to Paracelsus,

But Jones characteristically uses Paracelsus and others as materials to corroborate, confirm, and amplify his hypothesis. The meaning of "semen" remains that of a repressed sexual image. Although he devotes himself to the feminine-folklore, anthropology, history, and myth-it is his commitment to the male fertilizing principle and the myth of patriarchy that gives his text its precarious tension. Jones's text is overrun with examples which, if often fascinating, are excessive and far outweigh the purpose of demonstrating his stated goals. His relish for detail exhibits an almost fetishistic passion, "the pleasure lying in making the subject as complete as possible."[21] Yet his filial devotion to Freud and science seems to hold an upper hand. From another perspective, if Jones thought of himself as a son/lover in relation to Freud, then his anima possession reveals itself in his love for myth and symbol, for the unique and odd, for the customs and rites of the world's cultures. It is their presence as passionate obsession, though subjugated to logocentric ends, that expresses itself like the furies from the unspoken beneath the darkness of superstition. The Dionysian tumult of their exotic images is an objection to the repression of the scientific method. Any reader will be seduced and lured by these intriguing examples, but the senses are soon dulled by the extent to which they are used. In a sense, Jones's essay is like all alchemical monstrum—a premature, unholy marriage of domination, a beautifully grotesque antique of early psychoanalysis, but like the monsters of ancient myth, fascinating and compelling as if the unfulfilled promise of imaginal revelation is waiting to be born.

"the whole of the Microcosm is potentially contained... and in which is contained the nature, quality, character, and essence of beings, and which ethereal life-fluid in man may be looked upon as invisible or hidden man" (ibid., 71).

21. *The Complete Correspondence of Sigmund Freud and Ernest Jones*, 62. Also on 15 March 1912 Jones writes, "The type of work I like doing is that of taking a small subject that can be covered completely such as Salt Symbolism and dealing with it fully" (ibid., 136).

II. *Salt as the Arcane Substance:* Aura Seminalis *and the Erotics of Lunar Symbolism*

While Freud and Jones privileged logos over Eros, in Jung, submerged Eros returns with scholarly and imaginative force.[22] His reflection on the image of salt begins with a fundamentally different approach from Jones. For Jung the image of salt, as all images, requires a fundamental respect for its context to be properly understood, and it is to this context that the meaning of the image is initially referred, and perhaps fundamentally, deferred. While both Jung and Jones place the image of salt in a variety of contexts, Jung lingers over the lessons inherent in each example rather than using the collective examples to reach unifying conclusions. For Jones contextual meaning is instrumental proof of a general theory that suggests a latent meaning for the metaphor of salt. For Jung, contextual citations serve as amplifications of the image of salt. This is part of his method, necessary "in order to do justice to the various aspects of the unconscious that are expressed by salt."[23]

Beginning with his theory of *correspondentia* axiomatic in the Middle Ages, Jung begins by placing salt in alchemical contexts. "The method of alchemy," he says, "psychologically speaking, is one of boundless amplification." The amplification or *"amplificatio* is always appropriate when dealing with some dark experience which is so vaguely adumbrated that it must be enlarged and expanded by being set in a psychological context in order to be understood at all."[24]

---

22. Jung's reflections on salt are contained in his last great work, *Mysterium Coniunctionis (CW14)*, originally published in German in 1955–56. It contains Jung's reflections on the alchemical soul and was completed in his eightieth year. It has been considered by many to be his most arcane and complex contribution to a psychological understanding of alchemy and to a comprehensive understanding of his vision and work. His reflections on salt are contained in ch. 3, "The Personification of Opposites," and follows his discussion of lunar symbolism. A very helpful discussion of the above is contained in Edward F. Edinger's *The Mysterium Lectures: A Journey through C. G. Jung's* Mysterium Coniunctionis, transcribed and edited by Joan Dexter Blackmer (Toronto: Inner City Books, 1995).

23. *CW*14, par. 234.

24. *CW*12, par. 403. Also see *CW*3, par. 413: "Even the most individual systems are not absolutely unique, but offer striking and unquestionable analogies with other

For him, the image is initially dark and ambiguous, a mystery which, when placed in context, enlarges and differentiates itself so it can be seen in a more variegated way. Common similarities of form give relief to the psychological structure in which the mystery is embedded. The result is a metaphoric, symbolic, and psychological sense of what is revealed by the unconscious. For Jung, the symbol is not a word or concept, a clear and distinct idea, but rather an image pointing to other images, a range of images that can not yet be formulated in any other or better way.

Jung argues that various aspects of the unconscious are expressed by salt.[25] His reflections begin in a chapter concerned with the notion of opposites and their union, and follow a section devoted to lunar symbolism in which salt is a "special instance."[26] Jung places salt in the alchemical triad of *Sulphur-Mercurius-Sal* where it is found that Mercurius partakes of both masculine (red, sulphur) and feminine (lunar, sal). If Jones finds his "seminal substance " confined to the masculine, Jung finds it beyond gender, an arcane substance closer to the understanding of Paracelsus. Jung states that "Mercurius, however, is not just the medium of conjunction but also that which is to be united, since he is the essence or 'seminal matter' of both man and woman."[27] Jung explains that Mercurius "usually stands for the arcane substance, whose synonyms are the panacea and the 'spagyric medicine'... [T]he latter [is identified] with the 'balsam' of Paracelsus, which is...to be found in the human body and is a kind of aetheric substance,"[28] or, we might say, an imaginal substance.

Sal is ultimately traced by Jung to both masculine and feminine identifications and eventually found in all things. He quotes Hermes: "Our salt is found in a certain precious Salt, and in all things. On this account

---

systems. From the comparative analysis of many systems the typical formulations can be discovered. If one can speak of reduction at all, it is simply a reduction to general types, but not to some general principle arrived at inductively or deductively, such as 'sexuality' or 'striving for power.' This paralleling with other typical formulations serves only to widen the basis on which the construction is to rest."

25. *CW* 14, par. 234.

26. Ibid.

27. Ibid., par. 659.

28. Ibid., par. 663.

GEBER ARABS
Philofophús.

Fig. 3 An emblem of the medieval Islamic alchemist Jābir ibn Hayyān (lat. Geber) with the motto "Everything in nature is in Sun and Salt."

the ancient Philosophers called it the common moon."[29] While primarily related to lunar psychology, philosophical alchemy employed salt as a cosmic principle. Yet due to its radically paradoxical nature, Jung traced it as one of the designations for the "Arcane Substance."[30] Jung amplifies his supposition by noting salt's appearance in the early Middle Ages, where under Arabic influence salt water is a synonym for the *aqua permanens.* Jung quotes Seniors' unequivocal statement that "Mercurius is made from salt."[31] In Latin alchemy, "Sal Alkali" plays the role of the arcane substance[32] and in the "Allegoriae Sapientum," the lapis is described as "salsus" (salty).[33] Jung finds even clearer associations among later alchemists, such as Mylius, in whose writing salt is synonymous with the tincture, the earth dragon who eats his own tail and the "ash...the diadem of the heart."[34] Basilius Valentinus speaks of *sal spirituale* and defines it as "the seat of virtue which makes the 'art' possible...it is the 'quintessence, above all things and in all creatures.'

---

29. Ibid., par. 255, n.383. The quotation from Hermes Jung notes as in the *Rosarium Philosophium* (*Art. aurif.,* 2: 244).

30. Ibid., par. 240.

31. Ibid. Recall also the relation of *aqua permanens* and *aqua pontica* (dirty water) as symbolic enlargements of the notion of urine in Jones. See *CW* 12, par. 338, fig. 121.

32. Ibid.

33. Ibid.

34. Ibid., par. 241.

'The whole magistery lies in the salt and its solution'... and is altogether a mystery to be concealed."[35] "As the arcane substance it is identified with various synonyms... [but] above all it is an 'ens centrale.'"[36]

Toward the end of *Mysterium Coniunctionis,* Jung asks: "What, then, do the statements of the alchemists concerning their arcanum mean, looked at psychologically?"[37] In order to answer this question he returns to his method for understanding dreams and his definition of a symbol as "the best possible formulation for still unknown or unconscious facts."[38] Thus for Jung the image of salt, while continuing to be differentiated, remains a symbolic mystery deferred, an arcanum of imagination, which he traces and amplifies in alchemy, classical mythology, Egyptian and Chinese religion, folk ideas, superstitions, and magical papyri, finding it to be an expression of male and female, light and dark, good and evil, black and white, typical of the bipolarity of an archetype.

The bipolarity of white and black belongs to salt, though the blackened aspect linking salt with the nigredo is rarely mentioned.[39] Jung traces the dark nature of salt in its "foetid smell," its relation to "malefic Saturn," and its "murderous quality."[40] For Jung whiteness, associated only with semen in Jones's essay, is seen symbolically in the images of the "white stone," "the white sun," "the full moon," "the fruitful white earth cleaned and calcined." As a white substance it is also the "white woman," "the salt of our magnesia and the spark of the *anima mundi*" or world soul.[41]

Linking the archetype with the imagination and the soul, Jung throws some light on the overlapping significations of salt. "[T]he obscurity begins to clear up when we are informed, further, that one of its principle meanings is *soul.*"[42] As soul, Jung equates salt with the "spark of

---

35. Ibid.

36. Ibid., par. 242.

37. Ibid., par. 772.

38. Ibid. Jung goes on to speak about his theory of compensation and the importance of the arcanum for a dissociated consciousness.

39. Ibid., par. 244.

40. Ibid., par. 338–39.

41. Ibid., par. 321. Jung notes that for the alchemists magnesia was as a rule the arcane substance and not a specific chemical one.

42. Ibid.

the *anima mundi*" and "daughter of the *spiritus vegetativus* of creation."[43] As a soul image, salt is associated with the anima and the feminine principle of "Eros, which brings everything into relationship."[44] Jung sees the work of Eros as necessary to bring the opposite dimensions of the arcanum into connection, and he focuses on two of the most outstanding properties that are brought together in the image of salt—bitterness and wisdom.[45] The factor common to both is the functioning of feeling:

> Tears, sorrow, and disappointment are bitter, but wisdom is the comforter in all psychic suffering. Indeed, bitterness and wisdom form a pair of alternatives: where there is bitterness wisdom is lacking, and where wisdom is there can be no bitterness. Salt, as the carrier of this fateful alternative, is coordinated with the nature of woman.[46]

For Jung the patriarchal mind split off from Eros can never achieve insight "without the participation of feeling."[47] Wisdom can come from bitterness only as a "differentiation of feeling," and it is differentiated feeling that begins to unify the opposites.[48] The work of unifying opposites requires a fundamental transformation, not simply an intellectual synthesis. It is a work of emotional engagement, of working in the dark and with the dark side of the psyche, with what Jung calls the shadow. According to Jung, Freud underestimated the difficulty of this type of transformation, for it takes far more than the ego as a rational mediator. "What [Freud] did not see was that the confrontation with the shadow is not just a harmless affair that can be settled by 'reason.'"[49]

---

43. Ibid., par. 322.

44. Ibid.

45. Ibid., par. 330.

46. Ibid.

47. Ibid., par. 332.

48. Ibid. par. 334. Charles Taylor critiques Jung for equating Eros with differentiated feeling, pointing out that Eros shoots the arrow that connects one person with another, but that he is masculine (not feminine), the assertive counterpart to the allure of Aphrodite. Eros has less to do with understanding and wisdom than has salt. "The suffering brought about by Eros connections may well lead to (if worked on) differentiated feeling but there is no assurance that it will" (Taylor, *Salt in Dreams and Psychotherapy*, 29).

49. *CW* 14, par. 342.

Jung sees the shadow as exerting "a dangerous fascination which can be countered only by another *fascinosum*."[50] This *fascinosum* is found by Jung in the inner life of man like a "spark of light" and "those laboring in the darkness must try to accomplish an opus that will cause the 'fishes' eyes' to shine."[51] He distinguishes this possibility of illumination from that of revelation, and suggests that this potent revelation "yields a 'bitter' water by no means acceptable to our human judgment."[52]

Jung connects this alchemical insight to the process of analysis and to the process of making the unconscious conscious:

> It is bitter indeed to discover behind one's lofty ideals narrow, fanati-cal convictions, all the more cherished for that, and behind one's heroic pretensions nothing but crude egotism, infantile greed, and complacency. This painful corrective is an unavoidable stage in every psychotherapeutic process.[53]

While "Freud halted the process at the reduction to the inferior half of the personality," Jung's notion of transformation included a vision of the Self.[54] The idea of wholeness held the tension of the radical opposites and produced a transcendent possibility not unlike the alchemist's idea of the lapis, philosopher's stone, or arcane substance. Quoting Khun-rath, Jung notes that salt is seen to have the "paradoxical double nature of the arcane substance," an image containing the "most potent opposites imaginable" for which reason it was also called the Rebis.[55]

Jung found that the meaning of salt is not found in common salt. By following its multiple contexts, the image is enlarged, amplified, poly-valent, and radically deferred, reflecting various aspects of the uncon-scious. It is a symbolic, psychological and imaginal substance, an instance of lunar symbolism, an aetheric and cosmic principle. As such, it is far more than a mental, rational principle, but constitutes an *ens centrale*, an embodiment of the alchemical soul, a principle of Eros and

---

50. Ibid., par. 343.
51. Ibid., par. 345.
52. Ibid., par. 346.
53. Ibid.
54. Ibid.
55. Ibid., par. 337.

the Self. In moving from Jones to Jung, we go from salt as an image of "semen" to the *aura seminalis* whose potency is in the spark of the *anima mundi* creating not only literal life but a transcendent possibility. By viewing all these meanings together, Jung felt he approached a clarified vision of the whole. He noted that "the sum of all these statements is seldom or never ... formulated in any one author."[56] In the end, Jung considered his method a circular art and follows Olympidorus who stated: "Thus the key to the meaning of circular art is the synopsis thereof."[57]

Fig. 4 Mercurius as "uniting symbol," from Basilius Valentinus, *The Twelve Keys*, in *Musaeum Hermeticum* (1678).

56. Ibid., par. 335. Jung does not use the term *aura seminalis*, but it is another image of the arcane substance and shows how an expanding and symbolic notion of semen can be seen from a Jungian point of view.

57. Ibid., par. 335, n. 661.

III. *Salt: The Dissemination and Fervor of the Alchemical Soul*

If Jung's approach to salt emphasized a scholarly method of amplification, and Jones relied on association, Hillman executes a stylistic shift. His intention is less to extent a psychology of alchemy than to develop an alchemical way of psychologizing and restoring an alchemical mode of imagining. In this not untypical turn of phrase, Hillman twists psychology in such a way that it activates the image and the imagined use of analogy, giving depth to daily experiences.[58] While Jung and Jones have examined salt "in a scholarly manner in order to give an objective meaning," Hillman attempts to "bring over to the reader its substantiality as a commonly recognizable experience." This shift in pedagogy, while bearing similarities to both the phenomenological and postmodern traditions, does not fall easily into any category and is best understood in the context of his position on alchemical language.

Hillman's approach contributes to and departs from the Jungian tradition. On the one hand Hillman wants to deliteralize our abstract "concepts, distinguishing between words and things," while on the other to "re-materialize our concepts giving them body, sense, and weight."[59] For Hillman alchemy's beauty lies in its "materialized language which can never be taken literally."[60] The point here is not to simply restore the "neologisms" of alchemical language as literal but, rather, to restore a way of imagining and returning matter to our speech.[61]

---

58. Hillman notes that "Freud's method of associating all through memory, or Jung's method of amplifying all through history and culture...each have the effect of losing the image." See his "An Inquiry into Image," *Spring: An Annual of Archetypal Psychology and Jungian Thought* (1977): 86–87. Hillman's preference is for analogy that refers to a relation where there is a likeness in function but not in origin. Analogy like amplification can adumbrate an image and give it weight and extension, but unlike interpretation it does not posit a common origin of the similarities, such as semen, Eros, etc. Hillman feels that in Jung there is at times a tendency to press for an underlying structure while his emphasis is to keep the image alive and well by returning to it each time for a fresh sense of it. See *A Blue Fire: Selected Writings by James Hillman*, edited by Thomas Moore (New York: Harper Collins, 1989), 244–45, for a discussion of analogy.

59. James Hillman, "The Therapeutic Value of Alchemical Language: A Heated Introduction," in *UE5: Alchemical Psychology*, 16.

60. Ibid.

61. Ibid., 18.

Salt for Hillman "matters," and he begins with it as a psychological, metaphorical substance and archetypal principle. He activates the image and, like Jung, traces it in alchemical texts, finding those "qualities of human life [that] belong to the very substance of character." His model is a microcosmic/macrocosmic approach which asks that we enter the world of matter using our senses to find qualitative differences, and that we find metaphors or analogies of physical processes in our experience (ibid.).

> The work of soul-making requires corrosive acids, heavy earths, ascending birds; there are sweating kings, dogs and bitches, stenches, urine, and blood...
>
> ...I know that I am not composed of sulphur and salt, buried in horse dung, putrefying or congealing, turning white or green or yellow, encircled by a tail-biting serpent, rising on wings. And yet I am! I cannot take any of this literally, even if it is all accurate, descriptively true.[62]

Thus "salts belong to the very stuff of the psyche. *Sal* describes one of our matters," and this matter is formed by descent into the experiential component of the body in its "blood, sweat, tears, and urine." Developing Jung's idea that salt refers to Eros, Hillman says that salt is the "objective ground of personal experience, making experience possible." That is, salt makes events sensed and felt, giving taste and flavor, underlining that these events are both common and yet mine. In other words, salt acts like the "ground of subjectivity," and as subjects we are always subjected to our experiences.

When subjected to pain and suffering, our subjectivity can become initiatory. Alchemy for Hillman helps to differentiate kinds of suffering. Salt refers to those experiences which are sharp, stinging, and acute, and burn with wit and bite. They can be corrosive, acrimonious, and make sense through self-accusation and self-purification. Salt is purgative. Lead, by contrast, is "chronic and dense, heavy and oppressive, a gloomy kind of suffering without a specified focus, senseless...constipative." "Where salt tastes the details of its pain by remembering precisely and with piercing agony, lead cannot see." Hillman notes that the curing of these conditions

---

62. Hillman, "The Therapeutic Value of Alchemical Language," 13, 16.

also differs, "where salt requires a pinch, often feeling the pinch of the events that sting, lead seems to require time."

Going beyond our traditional understanding of healing, Hillman points to the fact that, in the light of alchemy, felt experience takes on a different meaning. Through it we can imagine our deep hurts not only as "wounds to be healed but as salt mines from which we gain a precious essence and without which the soul cannot live." Hillman asserts: "we make salt in our suffering. By working through our sufferings, we gain salt, healing the soul of its salt-deficiency." This seems to be why we fix-ate on our wounds and why we are drawn back again and again to our childhood hurts. Pain brings us both to our body and to the body psyche. We have a need to look back, says Hillman, and it is in this looking back that we create salt and soul.

Fig. 5 An illustration of Lot's wife turning into a statue of salt by Gustave Doré, from *The Doré Bible Gallery* (Chicago: Belford-Clarke Co., 1891).

One paradigmatic story of looking back, Hillman notes, is that of Lot's wife (Genesis 19:26). Though there are a number of interpreta-tions, Jewish and Christian commentators have referred to looking back as an act of searching for those who have been left behind. It is the result-ing bitterness of separation and loss that can overwhelmingly turn one to salt. In lesser ways, "family fixations are also salt-mines. The disap-pointments, worries, smarts of mother-complex love—the evening with the photograph album, the keepsakes—are ways the psyche produces salt." The danger here lies in fixation. The stuff that creates a sense of subjectivity and the life of the soul can also be that by which our lives are stuck and even destroyed. Too much or too little salt is problematic for the soul.[63]

The fixative quality of salt is not simply negative. Hillman gives a number of striking examples from dreams and situations dealing with themes of youthful impulsivity: carelessness, young love, lovers' fights, and even studying for exams. These examples enact stages of the salt/sulphur conjunction, where salt is said to wound or slay impulsivity (sulphur). This action on sulphur in right proportion helps to preserve relationships and build structure. "We need salt in microcosmic ecology for fixing, toughening, preserving." Salt acts to integrate the personality, to coagulate our alienated driftings, to vitalize our flatness and to ground our "winged speculations " in tangibility. These psychological movements take place not only in the conscious application of wisdom but in autonomous psychic movement. "The soul forces its tangibility upon us and brings home our common and base susceptibility to human pain."[64]

Hillman has activated the image of salt, following its analogies in metaphor and archetypal principle in the materiality of psyche and in psyche's personal and common experiences. He has found it an alchemical substance that gives flavor and taste to experience. It is through salt that we experience our pain and suffering. It is a substance that requires the right dosage, and in proper relation to other elementals, it can build structure, integrate, ground, and vitalize our lives. From the wisdom of Paracelsian medicine to the literature of D.H. Lawrence, Hillman pursues the fervor of salt, and it is this fervor which becomes the focus of the last section of his paper.

Jones's fervor led him to semen and Jung's to the *aura seminalis*; Hillman finds fervor in dissemination. Although Hillman does not use the word dissemination, the term characterizes an aspect of his style that flavors his work. As defined by Barbara Johnson, dissemination "is what subverts all...recuperative gestures of mastery. It is what foils the attempt

---

63. Both Hillman and Taylor note the importance of the right amount of salt being a critical factor.

64. Hillman reflects that perhaps Jung is writing about Eros.

to progress in an orderly way toward meaning or knowledge, what breaks the circuit of intentions or expectations through some ungovernable excess."[65]

If Jones's passion is for cutting below and Jung's is for finding unification of opposites, then Hillman's is for differentiation and particularization: "Salt requires particularization, it forces one to take note of the specific taste of each event, tangibility means recognition and discrimination of specific natures." It would seem that this move toward particularization is precisely what works against the inherent tendency of salt to "knot and cement." For Hillman it is "the very nature of salt to literalize and conserve itself into a crystal body." This aspect of salt effects the way it is discussed. Writings about salt tend to "conclude with a clotted thought, a reduction to a basic idea," such as semen or Eros. While both Jones and Jung spill salt out into multiple contexts, their approaches tend to congeal. Even in Jung's approach of highly polysemic amplification, Hillman finds a tendency to press toward a master trope leading to an over valued idea (Eros) symbolically representing the overcoming of opposites.

Hillman's discussion of this tendency in Jung bears a resemblance to the work of Jacques Derrida. Both critique the move from highly particularized multiplicity toward any teleological and transcendent function and unitary resumption of meaning. For Hillman as well as Derrida

> polysemia or polythematism doubtlessly represents progress in relationship to the linearity of the monothematic writing or reading that is always anxious to anchor itself to the tutelary meaning, the *principal* signified of a text, that is, its major referent. Nevertheless, polysemia, as such, is organized within the implicit horizon of a unitary resumption of meaning, that is, within the horizon of a dialectics...that at a given moment, however far off, must permit reassemblage of the totality of a text into the truth of its meaning.[66]

---

65. "Translator's Introduction," in Jacques Derrida's *Dissemination,* translated by Barbara Johnson (Chicago: The University of Chicago Press, 1981), xxxii.

66. "Positions: Interview with Jean-Louis Houdebine and Guy Scarpetta," in Jacques Derrida, *Positions,* translated by Alan Bass (Chicago: The University of Chicago Press, 1981), 45.

In that polythematism or polytheism remains within a dialectical movement toward wholeness or unity, it loses its generative multiplicity. Thus for Hillman any insight or experience presented as truth or faith closes in on itself and becomes "virginal." Even the "salt of wisdom (*sal sapiantia*)...[can] become crystallized and destructive when taken alone."

Hillman believes this destructive aspect of salt takes place when salt is *in extremis,* when by its own "lethal and volatile " nature it crystallizes into its own "inherent virginity" and thus fixates and moves toward an even purer essence. He notes that we can recognize this when "the principle of fixation has become a fixation of principle. Then salt is unable to be combusted...by sulfur...[and] neither life nor insight [is] possible, only dedication, fervid and pure."

It is in Hillman's refusal to nominalize and to depart from particularization, in his call to an irreducible generative multiplicity, that one can find the heaviest concentration of salt. If there is any place one feels the fervor of salt, it is in this aspect of his approach. He aims at both theoretical concerns and, perhaps even more poignantly, at the larger cultural, political, and doctrinal affairs, where an overdose of salt shows itself in "puritanism, fanaticism, [and] terrorism."

For Hillman "society is always in danger of the fervor of salt," and it is his passion to subvert the destructive aspects of fixation wherever they occur. While there are strong resonances with postmodernism, the acid of Hillman's iconoclastic enthusiasm is mediated by an equally strong fundamental valuing of the concrete image and psychic need for substantiality. He is acutely aware of the hyperactivation of salt. Hillman warns us that "the dosage of salt is an art: it must be taken *cum grano salis,* not corrosive, bitter irony and biting sarcasm or fixed, immortal dogma, but the deft touch that brings out the flavor."

If at times its saltiness overwhelms the reader, the insights in this essay never homogenize and congeal. Hillman's text continually self-deconstructs. His iconoclasm turns on itself so that the result, while never without substance, does not harden into a dogma but serves as a vessel of soul making.[67]

---

67. The clearest statement of Hillman's self-deconstructive style is from *Re-visioning Psychology* (New York: Harper & Row, 1975), 229:

Conclusion

In reflecting on these three essays, it is interesting to consider the perspective of Richard Rorty who characterized scientific thinking as a successive development of new languages, metaphors, and vocabularies. While the authors focus mainly on salt, they say something about method, approach, and the nature of the human soul. In each there are different understandings of salt, as well as multiple approaches for reaching that understanding. In soul-making and the making of depth psychology, literal "truth " has been de-emphasized and displaced by a perspectival approach. Salt serves as a Nietzschean example of truth perceived in terms of a multiplicity of metaphors.[68]

Rorty likewise has come to see that the "human self is created by the use of a vocabulary rather than being adequately or inadequately expressed in a vocabulary" and, for the most part, "truth is made rather than found."[69] In this spirit, one might read the following essays as "metaphoric redescriptions rather than insight into nature.[70] Mary Hesse described such

---

Though this has been a groundwork of irreplaceable insights, they are to be taken neither as foundations for a systematic theory nor even as a prolegomenon for any future archetypal psychology. Soul-making needs adequate ideational vessels, and it equally needs to let go of them. In this sense all that is written in the foregoing pages is confessed to with passionate conviction, to be defended as articles of faith, and at the same time disavowed, broken, and left behind. By holding to nothing, nothing holds back the movement of soul-making from its ongoing process, which now like a long Renaissance processional slips away from us into memory, off-stage and out of sight…and when the last image vanishes, all icons gone, the soul begins again to populate the stilled realms with figures and fantasies born of the imaginative heart.

See also William Kerrigan speaking of Derrida: "Because of the new demands of his peculiar (and I think, unusually scrupulous) intellectual integrity require him to occupy and vacate positions simultaneously." "Atoms Again: The Deaths of Individualism," in *Taking Chances: Derrida, Psychoanalysis and Literature,* edited by Joseph H. Smith and William Kerrigan (Baltimore and London: The Johns Hopkins University Press, 1984), 86.

68. Richard Rorty, *Contingency, Irony and Solidarity* (New York: Cambridge University Press, 1989), 27.

69. Ibid., 7.

70. Ibid., 16. In the above, Rorty is following the thought of Mary Hesse's "The

redescriptions as the stuff of scientific revolutions. Rorty also notes the Kuhnian point that "even in the sciences, metaphoric redescriptions are the mark of genius and of revolutionary leaps forward."[71]

If this orientation is credible in the natural sciences, it is that much more so for the genres of depth psychology. It is interesting to consider depth psychology less in terms of a development toward truth than as a field of archetypal perspectives. Nietzsche's definition of truth, writes Rorty, "amounted to saying that the whole idea of 'representing reality' by means of language, and thus the idea of finding a single context for all human lives, should be abandoned."[72]

In reprinting the following essays here, it is not the intention to juxtapose them to decipher the true meaning of salt nor to favor any depth psychological approach but, rather, to recognize and appreciate a particular genius. Derrida has noted that as long as criticism attempts to decide on the truth or meaning of a text, it is operating within the horizon of metaphysical thought.[73]

For Rorty, it "somehow became possible, toward the end of the nineteenth century, to take the activity of redescription more lightly than it had ever been taken before. It became possible to juggle several descriptions of the same event [and image] without asking which one was right—to see redescription as a tool rather than a claim to have discovered essence."[74] This requires a spirit of playfulness that allows for alternative descriptions and overrides the demand for "The One Right

---

Explanatory Function of Metaphor," in Mary Hesse, *Revolutions and Reconstructions in the Philosophy of Science* (Bloomington: Indiana University Press, 1980).

71. Rorty, *Contingency, Irony and Solidarity*, 28.

72. Ibid., 27.

73. Alan Bass notes that for Derrida criticism "derives from the Greek *krinein*, to *decide*. All criticism, thus far, has been programmed by the metaphysical *decision* to value truth, presence, meaning...Speculative dialectics aims to master, to unify and to reappropriate contradiction. Truth is reached by negation and reconciliation." For Derrida, "the "illogic" that leaves the opposites unresolved represents a profound challenge to metaphysical thinking, that construes contradiction only in terms of resolution, in terms of *deciding* in the name of truth." "The Double Game," in *Taking Chances: Derrida, Psychoanalysis, and Literature*, 72–74.

74. Rorty, *Contingency, Irony and Solidarity*, 39.

Description."[75] This playfulness is essential if we are not to fall prey to the fervor of salt to congeal into a single-mindedness. Hillman states:

> Unless we are trained in the nature and power of salt, as were the alchemists and the Vestal Virgins, we become unwitting terrorists of the night, no matter how noble our dedication. Fanatical singleness frees one from the power of the other but at the expense of destroying the other's core existence.[76]

Both Jones and Jung have been critiqued for the tendency of their approaches to congeal. But we have seen that this tendency is inherent in the fervor of salt. This fervor was also evident in Hillman's passion for deconstruction.

Above and beyond these critiques, one cannot help but appreciate these authors for the richness of their contribution. Jones's particular appeal lies in his youthful enthusiasm, his dedication to Freud and the psychoanalytic charter, and his fervent commitment to science. He is passionate in his love of myth and symbol, and his devotion to collecting the odd customs and rites of antiquity is remarkable. These customs and rites are themselves part of a psychological gold mine, and his use of them as anthropological proofs marks his work as a fundamental example of applied psychoanalysis.

Jung's essay impresses us by going against the tide of its time. He open-mindedly investigates the most arcane of subjects with a sustained and mature scholarly force. One cannot help but admire his patience, his capacity to tolerate ambiguity, and his willingness to enter into the dark side of psyche and labor there until the "fish eyes shine." Jung's vision is transformative and revolutionary, and the enormity of his scholarship has created an impressive school of depth psychology. *Mysterium Coniunctionis* is a difficult but fundamental work, and his essay on salt is an intrinsic piece of that vision.

Finally, Hillman's essay on salt and the alchemical soul is an exemplary rendering of archetypal (and alchemical) psychologizing. It is representative of a new start, style, and genre of psychology. His insights mark a non-reductive imagining which forces a reconsideration of one's

---

75. Ibid., 40.

76. Hillman, "The Therapeutic Value of Alchemical Language," 77–78.

stance and makes one take note of the particulars of each image and situation. Hillman's work is admirable for its refusal of staleness in thought and its astute psychological and cultural criticism. His work opens a new chapter in cultural and depth psychology and is remarkable for its simultaneous iconoclasm and expression of a substantive psychology.

The grouping of these essays has not been to affirm some hierarchy or to impose any kind of order on them. From an archetypal point of view, sensitivity to a variety of perspectives tends to produce psychological insights and "to restore psychology to the widest, richest, and deepest volume so that it would resonate with soul."[77] In such an approach we find "vitality in tension, learn from paradox, gather wisdom by straddling ambivalence, and gain confidence in trusting the confusion that naturally arises from multiplicity."[78]

In the end, the seasons and seasoning of depth psychology are preserved in the salt. Each essay is meant to be read slowly and savored, to be enjoyed for the richness of its imagery as well as for insight into the styles of the imagination that have structured the different genres of depth psychology. Hopefully they will enrich and reward the reader and give range to the way psychological work is imagined. And the editing of these papers is intended to enhance this aim.

---

77. Hillman, *A Blue Fire*, 26.

78. Ibid., 38 (from commentary by Thomas Moore).

ERNEST JONES

The Symbolic Significance of Salt in Folklore and Superstition

I.

In the course of some highly suggestive remarks on the subject of superstition Freud writes: "I take it that this conscious ignorance and unconscious knowledge of the motivation of psychical accidents is one of the psychical roots of superstition."[1] He maintains in general that the undue significance attached by the superstitious to casual external happenings arises from associative connections that exist between these and important thoughts and wishes of which the subject is quite unaware, and that it constitutes a projection of the significance really belonging to these unconscious thoughts; the feeling of significance, therefore, is fully justified, though it has been displaced into a false connection. The object of the present communication is to examine in the light of this thesis one of the most familiar and widespread of superstitions—namely, the belief that it is unlucky to spill salt at the table. In doing so the endeavor will be made to use the inductive method only, that is to say, to construct hypotheses only when they appear to be legitimate inferences from definitely ascertained facts and then to test them in their capacity to resume the whole range of accessible evidence.

Two primary considerations may be mentioned at the outset. First that in all ages salt has been invested with a significance far exceeding that inherent in its natural properties, interesting and important as these are. Homer calls it a divine substance, Plato describes it as especially dear to the gods,[2] and we shall presently note the importance attached to it in religious ceremonies, covenants, and magical charms. That this should

---

1. Sigmund Freud, *Zur Psychopathologie des Alltagslebens (Über Vergessen, Versprechen, Vergreifen, Aberglaube und Irrtum)* (Berlin: Verlag von S. Karger, 1904), 82.

2. *Plutarch's Morals,* translated, corrected, and revised by William W. Goodwin, 5 vols. (Boston: Little, Brown, and Company, 1878), 3: 336–38.

have been so in all parts of the world and in all times shows that we are dealing with a general human tendency and not with any local custom, circumstance, or notion. Secondly, the idea of salt has in different languages lent itself to a remarkable profusion of metaphorical connotations, so that a study of these suggests itself as being likely to indicate what the idea has essentially stood for in the human mind, and hence perhaps the source of its exaggerated significance.

We may begin by considering the chief characteristic properties of salt that have impressed themselves on popular thought and have in this way become associated with more general ideas of an allied nature. Perhaps the most prominent of these is the *durability* of salt and its *immunity against decay*. On account of this property, salt was regarded as "emblematic of durability and permanence,"[3] and hence of eternity and immortality;[4] in the Middle Ages it was thought that the devil for this reason detested salt.[5] In connection with eternity is also mentioned the idea of wisdom, which salt is likewise supposed to symbolize,[6] though Pitré says that this comes merely from a play on the words *sedes sapientia* and *sale e sapienza*.[7] Brand, however, quotes an introductory address delivered at a German university in the seventeenth century that seems to show an intrinsic connection between the two ideas: "The sentiments and opinions both of divines and philosophers concur in making salt the *emblem of wisdom or learning*; and that not only on account of what it is composed of, but also with respect to the several uses to which it is applied. As to its component parts, as it consists of the purest matter, so ought wisdom to be pure, sound, immaculate, and incorruptible; and similar to the effects which salt produces upon bodies ought to be those

---

3. Robert Means Lawrence, *The Magic of the Horse-Shoe with Other Folk-Lore Notes* (London: Gay and Bird, 1898), 157.

4. Siegfried Seligmann, *Der böse Blick und Verwandtes: Ein Beitrag zur Geschichte des Aberglaubens aller Zeiten und Völker*, 2 vols. (Berlin: Hermann Barsdorf Verlag, 1909), 2 : 33.

5. Jean Bodin, *De la Demonomanie des Sorciers* (Antwerp: J. Keerberg, 1593), 278.

6. J. Collin de Plancy, *Dictionnaire Infernal* (Paris: Paul Mellier, 1844), 441 (s.v. "Sel"); Lawrence, *The Magic of the Horse-Shoe*, 175.

7. Guiseppe Pitré, *Usi e costumi credenze e pregiudic del popolo Siciliano*, 4 vols. (Palermo: L. Pedone Lauriel di Carlo Clausen, 1889), 3 : 426.

of wisdom and learning upon the mind."[8] This explanation of the association between the ideas of salt and wisdom sounds a little too strained to
be altogether convincing and suggests that perhaps there may be other
determining factors besides those just mentioned. Wisdom was frequently
personified holding a salt-cellar, and the bestowal of *Sal Sapientia,* the Salt
of Wisdom, is still a formality in the Latin Church. The heavenly Sophia
appears in mystical science as sodium, and her color is yellow, the color of
burning salt.[9]

The idea of durability in regard to salt is evidently an important
cause of the old association between it and the topic of *friendship* and
loyalty.[10] Owing to its lasting and incorruptible quality it was regarded
as the emblem of perpetual friendship,[11] and from this several secondary meanings are derived. One corollary, for instance, is that the spilling
of salt is supposed to involve a quarrel or breaking of friendship.[12] Salt
has played an important part in matters of *hospitality.* Stuckius[13] tells us
that the Muscovites thought a prince could not show a stranger a greater
mark of affection than by sending to him salt from his own table. In Eastern countries it is a time-honored custom to place salt before strangers
as a token and pledge of friendship and good-will,[14] and in Europe it
was usually presented to guests before other food to signify the abiding
strength of friendship.[15] When an Abyssinian desires to pay an especially
delicate attention to a friend or guest he produces a piece of rock salt and

----

8. John Brand, *Observations on the Popular Antiquities of Great Britain,* 3 vols. (London: George Bell and Sons, 1877), 1 : 433.

9. Harold Bayley, *The Lost Language of Symbolism: An Inquiry into the Origin of Certain
Letters, Words, Names, Fairy-Tales, Folklore, and Mythologies,* 2 vols. (London: Williams
and Norgate, 1912), 1 : 228.

10. See Victor Hehn, *Das Salz: Eine kulturhistorische Studie* (Berlin: Gebrüder Born-
traeger, 1901), 10–12.

11. Brand, *Observations on the Popular Antiquities,* 3: 162; Lawrence, *The Magic of the
Horse-Shoe,* 169, 171.

12. Adolf Wuttke, *Der deutsche Volksaberglaube der Gegenwart* (Berlin: Wiegandt &
Grieben, 1900,), 211; Brand, *Observations on the Popular Antiquities,* 3: 162.

13. Johann Wilhelm Stucki, *Antiquitatum Convivialium* (Amsterdam, 1690), 17.

14. Lawrence, *The Magic of the Horse-Shoe,* 156.

15. Ibid., 169.

graciously permits the latter to lick it with his tongue.[16] In the most diverse countries and at all ages, from Ancient Greece to modern Hungary, salt has been used to confirm oaths and compacts;[17] according to Lawrence, "in the East, at the present day, compacts between tribes are still confirmed by salt, and the most solemn pledges are ratified by this substance." Such compacts are inviolable, and in the same way "to eat a man's salt," a phrase still in current use, carries with it the obligation of *loyalty*; during the Indian mutiny of 1857 a chief motive of restraint among the Sepoys was said to have been the fact that they had sworn by their salt to be loyal to the Queen.[18] Byron, in *The Corsair,* refers to this group of beliefs as follows (vv. 724–27):

> Why dost thou shun the salt? that sacred pledge,
> Which, once partaken, blunts the sabre's edge,
> Makes even contending tribes in peace unite,
> And hated hosts seem brethren to the sight![19]

Closely allied to the preceding feature of incorruptibility is the capacity salt possesses of *preserving other bodies from decay*. It is generally supposed that this is the reason for the power salt has of warding off the devil and other malignant demons, who have a horror of it.[20] The same property has also greatly aided in establishing the association between salt and immortality; the connection is plainly seen in the Egyptian custom of using salt for embalming. It is one reason for the custom, obtaining until recently in every part of Great Britain, of placing salt on a corpse;[21]

---

16. Ibid., 188.

17. Matthias Jacob Schleiden, *Das Salz: Seine Geschichte, seine Symbolik und seine Bedeutung im Menschenleben* (Leipzig: Wilhelm Engelmann, 1875), 71–73; Lawrence, *The Magic of the Horse-Shoe,* 164–66.

18. John Jackson Manley, *Salt and Other Condiments* (London: William Clowes and Sons, 1884), 90.

19. Lord Byron, *The Corsair: A Tale* (London: John Murray, 1814), 37.

20. Moncure Daniel Conway, *Demonology and Devil-Lore,* 2 vols. (New York: Henry Holt and Company, 1879), 1:288; Thomas Morison, *Papatus, seu depravatae religionis origo et incrementum* (Edinburgh 1594), 154; Bodin, *De la Demonomanie des Sorciers,* 278.

21. John Graham Dalyell, *The Darker Superstitions of Scotland Illustrated from History and Practice* (Edinburgh: Waugh and Innes, 1834), 102; Wirt Sikes, *British Goblins: Welsh Folk-Lore, Fairy Mythology, Legends and Traditions* (London: Sampson Low,

usually earth was added, "the earth being an emblem of the corruptible body, the salt an emblem of the immortal spirit." In later years this was said to be done so as to prevent decomposition,[22] an idea probably akin to the original one. A Welsh elaboration of the custom was to place a plate of bread and salt over the coffin (the combination of bread and salt will be discussed later); the professional "sin-eater" of the district then arrived, murmured an incantation and ate the salt, thereby taking upon himself all the sins of the deceased.[23]

An important conception of salt is that of its constituting the *essence* of things, particularly of life itself. This seems to include two sub-ideas, those of necessary presence and of value respectively. The idea of ultimate essence no doubt underlies the Biblical phrase "Ye are the salt of the earth" (Matthew 5: 13) and in many other expressions it is used in the sense of aristocratic, quintessential, and the like.[24] In alchemy salt was considered to be one of the three ultimate elements out of which the seven noble metals were generated. Mercury symbolized the spirit, sulfur the soul, and salt the body; mercury represented the act of illumination, sulfur that of union, and salt that of purification. Herrick, in his *Hesperides,* ranks salt even more highly:

> The body's salt the soul is; which when gone,
> The flesh soon sucks in putrefaction.[25]

In Ancient Egypt salt and a burning candle represented life, and were placed over a dead body to express the ardent desire of prolonging the life of the deceased.[26] The following argument was employed by Latin writers, e.g., Plutarch: "After death all parts of the body fall apart. In life the soul maintains the parts intact and in connection with one another. In the same way salt maintains the dead body in its form and connection,

Marston, Searle, & Rivington, 1880), 328; Brand, *Observations on the Popular Antiquities,* 2: 234–35.

22. Brand and Sikes, *loc. cit.*

23. Sikes, *British Goblins,* 324, 326.

24. *Oxford English Dictionary,* 8: 59.

25. *Hesperides, or, Works Both Humane and Divine of Robert Herrick* (London: George Routledge and Sons, 1885), 258.

26. Morison, *Papatus,* 89.

thus representing-so to speak-the soul."[27] The culmination of eulogies, in which the idea of value is also prominent, is to be found in a treatise on salt, published in 1770, where the writer launches forth in impassioned style the most extravagant encomiums upon this substance, which he avers to be the quintessence of the earth. Salt is here characterized as a Treasure of Nature, an Essence of Perfection, and the Paragon of Preservatives. Moreover, whoever possesses salt thereby secures a prime factor of human happiness among material things.[28]

Salt is closely associated with the idea of *money* or *wealth,* and indeed this is one of the connotations of the word. Nowadays the implication is even of excessive or unfairly high value, as in the colloquial phrase "a salt or salty price;" similarly in French *il me l'a bien salé* means "he has charged me an excessive price." In commercial circles the expression "to salt a mine or property" means to add a small quantity of some valuable substance to it so as artificially to raise its selling price. In Ancient Rome soldiers and officials were paid in salt instead of money, whence (from *salarium*) the modern words *salaire* and salary and the phrase "to be worth one's salt"(= to be capable, to earn one's salary). A salt currency was in vogue in Africa in the sixth century, and in the Middle Ages this was so also in England,[29] as well as in China, Tibet, and other parts of Asia.[30] The name of the Austrian coin "Heller" is derived from an old German word for salt, "Halle."[31] The Montem ceremony at Eton,[32] which consisted in collecting money in exchange for salt, was continued until 1847. Salt-Silver was the term used to denote the money paid by tenants to their lord as a commutation for the service of bringing him salt from market.[33] In parts of Germany the game is played of placing some sand, some salt,

---

27. Ibid.

28. Elias Artista Hermetica [Friedrich Christoph Oetinger], *Das Geheimnis vom Salz, als dem Lebensbalsam und dem Schatz aller Schätze* (Stuttgart, 1770).

29. Brand, *Observations on the Popular Antiquities,* 1 : 436.

30. Schleiden, *Das Salz,* 68–70, 82.

31. Hehn, *Das Salz,* 90.

32. Brand, *Observations on the Popular Antiquities,* 1 : 433–40.

33. Wuttke, *Der deutsche Volksaberglaube,* 233.

and a green leaf on the table and making a blindfolded person grope for them; if he seizes the salt it denotes wealth.[34]

These and other considerations have invested the idea of salt in the popular mind with a sense of *general importance*. Waldron[35] states that in the Isle of Man "no person will go out on any material affair without taking some salt in their pockets, much less remove from one house to another, marry, put out a child, or take one to nurse, without salt being mutually exchanged; nay, though a poor person be almost famished in the streets, he will not accept any food you will give him, unless you join salt to the rest of your benevolence." To carry salt with one on moving to a new dwelling is a very widespread custom;[36] it is related that when the poet Burns, in 1789, was about to occupy a new house at Ellisland, he was escorted there by a procession of relatives in whose midst was carried a bowl of salt.[37] The Arabs of Upper Egypt, before setting out on a journey, burn salt to prevent ill-luck.[38] The laying of salt at the table was in the Middle Ages a tremendous ceremony. The other implements were disposed with minute care in their relation to the salt, which throughout was treated with special deference.[39] With the Romans it was a matter of religious principle that no other dish was placed upon the table until the salt was in position. Rank and precedence among the guests were precisely indicated by their seat above or below the salt and their exact distance from it. Schleiden remarks: "How great was the importance attached to salt is also seen from the fact that hardly a place existed in which salt was produced where this was not expressed in the name of the place, from the Indian Lavanápura ('salt castle') and the Austrian *Salzburg* to the Prussian 'Salzkotten' and the Scottish salt-coats."[40]

---

34. Brand, *Observations on the Popular Antiquities,* 1 : 403.

35. George Waldron and Willliam Harrison, *Description of the Isle of Man,* The Manx Society, vol. XI (Douglas, Isle of Man: The Manx Society, 1725), 187.

36. Wuttke, *Der deutsche Volksaberglaube,* 396.

37. Charles Rogers and J.C. Higgins, *The Book of Robert Burns: Genealogical and Historical Memoirs of the Poet, His Associates, and Those Celebrated in His Writings,* 3 vols. (Edinburgh: Grampian Club, 1891), 3 : 202.

38. John Lewis Burckhardt, *Travels in Nubia* (London: John Murray, 1822), 169.

39. Lawrence, *The Magic of the Horse-Shoe,* 197–205.

40. Schleiden, *Das Salz,* 70.

The high importance attaching to salt led to various magical powers being ascribed to it, and it has been very extensively employed in magical procedures. It could be used for these and other purposes by placing it on the tongue or by rubbing the body with it, but the favorite method was to dissolve it in water and bathe the person with this. The principal function of salt in this connection, like that of most other charms, was to ward off harm, chiefly by averting the influence of malignant spirits. Salt is almost universally thought to be abhorrent to evil demons, [41] the only exception I know of being in Hungarian folklore, where on the contrary evil beings are fond of salt.[42] Salt was always missing from the devil's and witches' banquets.[43] Salt has therefore been one of the staple charms against the power of the devil,[44] of magicians,[45] of witches,[46] of the evil eye,[47] and of evil influences in general;[48] such beliefs are found in countries so far apart as Arabia[49] and Japan.[50] Cattle are also protected against witch-craft in the same way.[51] In India and Persia one can even determine by

41. Bodin, *De la Demonomanie des Sorciers,* 278; Collin de Plancy, *Dictionnaire Infernal,* 277–78; Schleiden, *Das Salz,* 78.

42. Lawrence, *The Magic of the Horse-Shoe,* 159.

43. Thomas Wright, *Narratives of Sorcery and Magic from the Most Authentic Soruces,* 2 vols. (London: Richard Bentley, 1851), 1: 310.

44. Bodin and Collin de Plancy, *loc. cit.*

45. Jacob Grimm, *Deutsche Mythologie,* 4 vols. (Berlin: Ferd. Dümmlers Verlagsbuch-handung, 1875–78), 2: 876.

46. Friedrich S. Krauss, *Slavische Volksforschungen: Abhandlungen über Glauben, Ge-wohnheitsrechte, Sitten und Bräuche und die Guslarenlieder der Südslaven* (Leipzig: Wilhelm Heims, 1908), 39; Wilhelm Mannhardt, *Germanische Mythen, Forschungen* (Berlin: Ferdinand Schneider, 1858), 7; Seligmann, *Der böse Blick,* 2: 33; Wuttke, *Der deutsche Volksaberglaube,* 95, 258, 283; Grimm, *Deutsche Mythologie,* 4: 461.

47. Seligmann, *Der böse Blick,* 1: 312–13, 320, 331, 344, 346, 365, 377, 389; 2: 73, 144, 220, 376.

48. Lawrence, *The Magic of the Horse-Shoe,* 177.

49. Burckhardt, *Travels in Nubia,* 169.

50. Georges Bousquet, *Le Japon de nos jours et les échelles de l'Extrême Orient,* 2 vols. (Paris: Librairie Hachette, 1877), 1: 94; William Elliot Griffis, *The Mikado's Empire* (New York: Harper & Brother, 1876), 467, 470.

51. Seligmann, *Der böse Blick,* 2: 104, 241, 329; Wuttke, *Der deutsche Volksaberglaube,* 40, 435, 438; Krauss, *loc. cit.*

means of salt whether a given person has been bewitched or not.[52] Salt will also protect the fields from evil influences.[53] It was further used to prevent the souls of the dead from returning to earth and to secure them peace in Purgatory.[54]

These practices were performed with especial frequency with *children*. The custom of rubbing new-born infants with salt is referred to in the Bible (Ezekiel 16: 4). The use of salt to guard the newborn against evil demons and evil influences, either by placing a little on the tongue or by immersing the infant in salt and water, was in vogue throughout Europe from early times, and certainly antedated Christian baptism;[55] in France the custom lasted until 1408 of putting salt on children until they were baptized, when it was considered no longer necessary:[56] At the present day it is still placed in the cradle of the new-born child in Holland.[57] In Scotland it was customary to put salt into a child's mouth on entering a stranger's house for the first time.[58] Salt was also placed in the mouth of a new-born calf for similar purposes as with children.[59]

Salt has been extensively used for *medicinal purposes*. It was believed to have the function of both preventing[60] and curing[61] diseases, as was already commented on by Pliny, particularly those caused by occult influences. It is possible that the Latin word *salus* (= health), the earliest connotation of which was "well-preserved," was originally related to the word *sal*.

---

52. Seligmann, *Der böse Blick*, 1: 262, 264.

53. Ibid., 2: 374.

54. Wuttke, *Der deutsche Volksaberglaube*, 465, 472.

55. Conway, *Demonology and Devil-Lore*, 2: 217; Lawrence, *The Magic of the Horse-Shoe*, 174–75; Seligmann, *Der böse Blick*, 1: 34; Wuttke, *Der deutsche Volksaberglaube*, 382, 387.

56. Schleiden, *Das Salz*, 79.

57. *New York Times*, 10 November 1889.

58. Dalyell, *The Darker Superstitions of Scotland*, 96.

59. Seligmann, *Der böse Blick*, 1: 58; Wuttke, *Der deutsche Volksaberglaube*, 436, 443.

60. Wuttke, *Der deutsche Volksaberglaube*, 374.

61. Dalyell, *The Darker Superstitions of Scotland*, 98–99, 102; Lawrence, *The Magic of the Horse-Shoe*, 180; Seligmann, *Der böse Blick*,1: 278; Wuttke, *Der deutsche Volksaberglaube*, 336.

Another important function of salt was its use in furthering fecundity. As this obviously cannot have been derived from any natural property of the substance, it must represent some symbolic significance in harmony with the general importance attached to it. Schleiden makes the following interesting remarks in this connection:

> The sea was unquestionably the fructifying, creative element. Leaving aside the few marine mammals, the offspring of sea creatures are to be counted by thousands and hundreds of thousands. This was all the more easily ascribed to the salt of the sea, since other observations believed to have been made were connected with it. It was recalled that in dog-breeding the frequent use of salt increased the number of the progeny, and that on ships carrying salt the number of mice multiplied to such an extent as to give rise to the idea of parthenogenesis, i.e., to the view that mice could beget young without the cooperation of a male. The conviction was thus formed that salt must stand in a close relation to physical love, so that salt became the *symbol of procreation.*[62]

It was used in this connection in two ways, to promote fecundity and to avert barrenness or impotence. The latter is illustrated by Elisha's action of throwing salt into the fountain of Jericho (2 Kings 2: 21): "Thus saith the Lord, I have healed these waters; and for the future they shall not be the occasion either of death or barrenness."

It is only natural that the general importance attached to salt should have been reflected in the sphere of *religion,* and we find that this was so in a remarkable degree. Salt was an essential constituent of sacrificial offerings in Ancient Egypt,[63] as well as in Greece and Rome;[64] Brand says of the latter: "Both Greeks and Romans mixed salt with their sacrificial cakes; in their lustrations also they made use of salt and water, which gave rise in after times to the superstition of holy water." In Judaism we find descriptions of three different usages taught by the Bible. As in other countries, salt formed a necessary part of sacrificial offerings: "Every oblation of thy meat offering shalt thou season with salt; neither shalt thou suffer the salt of the covenant of thy God to be lacking from thy meat

---

62. Schleiden, *Das Salz,* 92–93.
63. Arrian, *De Expeditione Alexandri,* 3.1
64. Brand, *Observations on the Popular Antiquities,* 3: 161.

offering: With all thine offerings thou shalt offer salt" (Leviticus 2: 13).[65]
A covenant, especially a religious covenant, was ratified by means of salt:
"It is a covenant of salt for ever, before the Lord" (Numbers 18: 19); "The
Lord God of Israel gave the kingdom over Israel to David for ever, even
to him, and to his sons, by a covenant of salt" (2 Chronicles 13: 5). The
idea of a bond of loyalty through eating salt also occurs: the passage "we
have maintenance from the king's palace" (Ezra 4: 14) means literally
"we are salted with the salt of the palace."[66] The salt sources in Germany,
which later became associated with the doings of witches, had a considerable religious significance; Ennemoser[67] writes of them: "Their yield
was regarded as a direct gift of the near Divinity, and the winning and
distributing of the salt as a holy occupation-probably sacrifices and folk
festivities were connected with the drying of the salt."

In the Roman Catholic Church, salt was introduced for baptismal
purposes in the fourth century[68] and has played a prominent part there
ever since.[69]

We may now consider another attribute of salt which has given rise
to many symbolic connotations—namely, its peculiar taste. Seligmann[70]
says: "Salt is on account of its piquant power a life-furthering material,"
and he associates with this the beliefs in the influence exerted by salt
when it penetrates into other substances, e.g., bread, and also the belief
in its capacity to cure disease. This property of salt has been especially
connected with speech in various metaphorical ways. Lawrence[71] writes:
"Owing to the importance of salt as a relish, its Latin name *sal* came to
be general sense, wit or sarcasm...The characterization of Greece

---

65. In Job 1: 22, the literal rendering of the passage "In all this Job sinned not, nor
charged God foolishly" is "In all this Job sinned not, nor gave God unsalted" (Conway,
Demonology and Devil-Lore, 2: 150).

66. Lawrence, *The Magic of the Horse-Shoe*, 156.

67. Joseph Ennemoser, *Geschichte der Magie* (Leipzig: F. A. Brockhaus, 1844), 839.

68. Heino Pfannenschmid, *Das Weihwasser im heidnischen und christlichen Cultus unter
besonderer Berücksichtigung des germanischen Althertums* (Hannover: Hahn'sche Hofbuch-
handlung, 1869), 166.

69. See Lawrence, *The Magic of the Horse-Shoe*, 76.

70. Seligmann, *Der böse Blick*, 1: 278.

71. Lawrence, *The Magic of the Horse-Shoe*, 161. See also Schleiden, *Das Salz*, 91.

used metaphorically as signifying a savory mental morsel, and, in a as the 'salt of nations' is attributed to Livy, and this is probably the origin of the phrase 'Attic salt', meaning delicate, refined wit." A pungent or pithy remark or jest is termed salt,[72] as in such expressions as "there is no salt in his witticisms," though the use of the word in this sense is becoming obsolescent in English; in French a similar one obtains, in expressions such as *une épigramme salé, il a répandu le sel à pleins mains dans ses écrits*, etc. In the Biblical passage (Epistle to the Corinthians 4: 6) "Let your speech be always with grace, seasoned with salt " this connotation is probably present, as well as that previously mentioned of wisdom or sense. The same metaphor is also applied in a general way, apart from speech, as in denoting an insipid man as "having no sense or salt," lacking in piquancy or liveliness, just as in Latin the word *insalsus* (= unsalted) meant stupid. This metaphorical attribute of salt is evidently closely akin to the one previously mentioned of "essentialness."

A property of salt that has been extensively exploited by the popular imagination is the ease with which it *dissolves in water.* That a substance otherwise so durable should disappear when put into water and, though leaving no visible trace of its presence, should endow the water with its peculiar properties (capacity to preserve from decay, pungent taste, etc.) has always impressed the people as being a remarkable characteristic, and is perhaps partly responsible for the mysterious significance attaching to holy water. One obvious practical application, of which frequent use has been made, is to estimate the amount of moisture in the atmosphere by the varying avidity of salt for it. It has thus been quite rationally used to *foretell the weather.*[73] This foretelling capacity of salt has naturally been generalized far beyond its original sphere. Thus, according as a particular heap of salt remains dry or not it is concluded that a corresponding person will or will not survive the coming year, that a given undertaking will be successful or the reverse, and so on.[74]

Water is not the only substance into which salt can be absorbed with the production of peculiar changes. Indeed, the capacity of salt to *enter into combination with a second substance* may be regarded as one of its most

---

72. See *Oxford English Dictionary, loc. cit.*

73. Thomas Willsford, *Nature's Secrets* (London, 1658), 139.

74. Wuttke, *Der deutsche Volksaberglaube,* 231.

salient characteristics. The substance with which it is by far the most often associated in this way is *bread*. The combination of the two has been used for practically all the purposes enumerated above in connection with salt, and in folk beliefs the two are almost synonymous. Thus bread and salt are both absent from the devil's feasts;[75] the combination of them is potent against witches,[76] and against the evil eye;[77] it guards cattle against disease,[78] ensures a plentiful supply of milk,[79] and removes obstacles to the churning of butter.[80] It is equally efficacious with adults and infants. It is carried into a new dwelling to avert evil influences and to bring good luck;[81] in Hamburg nowadays this custom is replaced by that of carrying at processional times a cake covered with chocolate, in the form of a bread roll, and a salt-cellar of marzipan filled with sugar. The combination of salt and bread has also been extensively used to confirm oaths,[82] and is still so used in Arabia at the present day.[83]

Lastly may be mentioned the attribute of salt as a *means of purification*. That salt water possesses this quality in a high degree was observed at an early stage of civilization, and by Roman ladies it was actually regarded as a means of attaining beauty.[84] Especially in regard to the sea this feature has led to numerous poetical applications and also to the development of many superstitions. It is intelligible that this purifying attribute should have played an important part in the use of salt in religious cults, and this we find was so, notably in Egypt and Greece.[85] We shall return to the subject later on when discussing the relation of purification to baptism.

---

75. Grimm, *Deutsche Mythologie,* 2: 877.

76. Seligmann, *Der böse Blick,* 2: 37, 52, 93, 94; Grimm, *Deutsche Mythologie,* 4: 454; Wuttke, *Der deutsche Volksaberglaube,* 129, 282.

77. Wuttke, *Der deutsche Volksaberglaube,* 282; Seligmann, *Der böse Blick,* 1: 398; 2: 37–38, 93–94, 100, 250, 334.

78. Dalyell, *The Darker Superstitions of Scotland,* 100.

79. Seligmann, *Der böse Blick,* 2: 38; Dalyell, *loc. cit.*

80. Seligmann, *loc. cit.*

81. Ibid., 2: 37.

82. Thomas Dekker, *The Honest Whore* (London, 1616), sc. 13; "Oath of Bread and Salt," *Blackwood's Edinburgh Magazine* 1, no. 3 (June 1817): 236; Lawrence, *The Magic of the Horse-Shoe,* 164.

83. Lawrence, *The Magic of the Horse-Shoe,* 185.

84. Schleiden, *Das Salz,* 84.

85. Ibid., 84–85.

II.

We may now survey the facts just related. While it has only been possible in the allotted space to give relatively few examples of the numerous ways in which ideas concerning salt have played a part in folk belief and custom—it would need a special treatise to record them all—it is probable that the most prominent and typical of them have been mentioned; at all events no special selection whatever has been made, beyond relegating sexual ones to the background. It is hardly necessary to say that the grouping here adopted is unduly schematic, being one of convenience in presentation only; a given custom would mostly be dictated by interest in other properties of salt as well as the one under which it is here mentioned.

In regard now to the matter that formed our starting point—namely, the superstitious fear of spilling salt—it is plain that here a significance is attached to an act that does not inherently belong to it, and it is equally plain that the same is true of most of the customs and beliefs related above. There are two possible explanations that may be offered for this state of affairs. The *first* would run somewhat as follows. The present-day superstition has no meaning beyond an historical one; it is simply an instance of the tendency of mankind to retain traditional attitudes for no intelligible reason, and is an echo of the time when the idea of salt was properly invested with a greater psychical value than it now is. In former times the significance attached to the idea of salt that we now regard as excessive was not so, being justified in fact and to be accounted for quite naturally by the real importance of the substance. There is undeniably a certain amount of truth in this view. Salt, being a substance necessary to life and in some countries obtainable only with considerable difficulty, [86] was inevitably regarded as both important and valuable, though this consideration must lose much of its weight in regard to most parts of the world where the supply is plentiful. Again, the curious properties of salt, its preserving capacity, its power of penetrating other substances, etc., would naturally impress the primitive mind, and the view just described would doubtless try to account for the belief in its magical powers by

---

86. Lawrence, *The Magic of the Horse-Shoe,* 187.

pointing out that such minds work on a simpler plane of thought than do ours. To this argument, however, comparative psychology could object that, although this type of thought—just as that of children—certainly often differs from what we term rational thinking, careful investigation always shows that it is very far from being so bizarre and unintelligible as it may at first sight appear; the formation of illogical connections is not meaningless, but has a perfectly definite and comprehensible reason for it. The general criticism, therefore, that must be passed on this explanation is that while it adduces unquestionably important considerations these are only partly capable of accounting for the facts, and are inadequate as a complete explanation of them. Other factors must have been operative in addition to those just mentioned.

The *second* explanation would supplement the first by regarding the excessive significance attaching to the idea of salt as an example of what Wernicke called an *Überwertige Idee,* that is to say, an idea overcharged with psychical significance. Only some of this inherently belongs to the idea itself, the rest being of adventitious origin. Such processes are, of course, very familiar in daily life: a bank note, for instance, is valued not for the intrinsic worth of the paper but for the worth that extrinsic circumstances give it. Psychoanalytic investigation has shown on the one hand that such transference of affect from one idea to another allied one is much commoner than was previously realized, and on the other hand that very often the subject is quite unaware of the occurrence. Thus a person may experience an intense affect—fear, horror, etc.—in regard to a given idea or object purely through the idea having formed strong associative connections with another idea which is justifiably invested with this affect; the intrinsic attributes of the idea do not account for the strong affect attached to it, this being in the main derived from a different source. The most striking manifestations of this process are seen in the psychoneuroses; the patient has a terror of a certain object which is not customarily regarded with terror, the reason being that the idea of the object is unconsciously connected in his mind with that of another object in regard to which the terror is quite comprehensible. In such cases the secondary idea may be said to represent or symbolize the primary one.[87]

---

87. For the precise distinction between symbolism and other forms of indirect

The more bizarre and apparently unintelligible is the phobia or other symptom, the more strained is as a rule the connection between it and the original idea, and the stronger is the emotion investing the latter. Apart from the neuroses, instances of exceedingly strained connections are less common. What happens as a rule is that the affect belonging to the two ideas, the symbolized and the symbolizing one, is very similar, so that the affect transferred from the one to the other accounts for only part of the affect accompanying the secondary idea. In this case the intrinsic qualities of the idea account for some of the affect, but not for all; the affect is appropriate in quality, but disproportionate in quantity. Unless the cause of this exaggeration is appreciated there is an unavoidable tendency to overlook the fact itself on rationalistic grounds; then the intrinsic qualities of the secondary idea are erroneously regarded as constituting an adequate explanation of the affect in question.

The main difference, therefore, between the two explanations is this: the first assumes that the affect, or psychical significance, attaching to the idea of salt was once not disproportionate to its real value, whereas the second, regarding the affect as disproportionate, maintains that some of it must be derived from an extraneous source.

In seeking for this source we have two distinct clues to guide us. In the first place, the universality of the beliefs and customs under discussion, and the remarkably high and even mystical significance that has been attached to the idea of salt, indicate that any further idea from which this may have been derived must be both a general one, common to all mankind, and one of fundamental psychical importance. In the second place, the association between the idea of salt and any further one must have been formed through the resemblances, real or fancied, of the corresponding qualities of the two ideas. It becomes necessary, therefore, to consider with closer attention the popular conception of these qualities that was described above.

This conception may be summarized as follows. Salt is a pure, white, immaculate and incorruptible substance, apparently irreducible into any further constituent elements, and indispensable to living beings. It has

mental representation, see ch. 7 of my *Papers on Psycho-Analysis* (Toronto: The Macmillan Company of Canada, 1918), "The Theory of Symbolism."

correspondingly been regarded as the essence of things in general, the quintessence of life, and the very soul of the body. It has been invested with the highest general significance—far more than that of any other article of diet—was the equivalent of money and other forms of wealth, and its presence was indispensable for the undertaking of any enterprise, particularly any new one. In religion it was one of the most sacred objects, and to it were ascribed all manner of magical powers. The pungent, stimulating flavor of salt, which has found much metaphorical application in reference to pointed, telling wit or discourse, doubtless contributed to the conception of it as an essential element; to be without salt is to be insipid, to have something essential lacking. The durability of salt, and its immunity against decay, made it an emblem of immortality. It was believed to have an important influence in favoring fertility and fecundity, and in preventing barrenness; this idea is connected with other attributes than the one just ·mentioned, probably indeed with them all. The permanence of salt helped to create the idea that for one person to partake of the salt of another formed a bond of lasting friendship and loyalty between the two, and the substance played an important part in the rites of hospitality. A similar application of it was for confirming oaths, ratifying compacts, and sealing solemn covenants. This conception of a bond was also related to the capacity salt has for combining intimately with a second substance and imparting to this its peculiar properties, including the power to preserve against decay; for one important substance—namely, water—it had in fact a natural and curious affinity.

If we now try to discover what other idea these ideas could arise in reference to, besides that of salt, the task is surely not difficult. If the word salt had not been mentioned in the preceding description anyone accustomed to hidden symbolism, and many without this experience, would regard it as a circumlocutory and rather grandiloquent account of a still more familiar idea—that of human semen. In any case a substance possessing the attributes just mentioned would lend itself with singular facility to such an association. Indeed, the mere fact that salt has been regarded as the emblem of immortality and wisdom is in itself suggestive to anyone who is alive to such possibilities, for the other well-known emblem of these two concepts is the snake, which is in mythology and elsewhere the phallic symbol *par excellence*. The surmise that the idea of salt has derived much of its significance from its being unconsciously associated with that of semen fulfills at least one postulate of all symbolic thinking—namely, that the idea from which the excessive significance is derived is more important psychically than the idea to which this is transferred; the radiation of the affect, like that of electricity, is always from the site of more intense concentration to that of less.

At the present stage of our investigation it is plain that the inference just drawn cannot be regarded as being much more than a surmise, or at the most a working hypothesis, one which will appear more or less plausible according to the experience of unconscious symbolism by which it is viewed. It must next be tested by the ordinary rules of science—namely, by its capacity to predict and by its power of satisfactorily reducing to simple terms a series of disparate phenomena.

If the hypothesis is correct then one could foretell that customs and beliefs would be found showing a direct relation between the idea of salt on the one hand and such ideas as those of marriage, sexual intercourse, and potency on the other, as well as a larger number showing a plainly symbolical relation between the two sets of ideas; further, that the ideas concerning salt and water mirror similar, more primitive ones concerning semen and urine, and that the partaking of salt would be connected with ideas relating to sexual intercourse and impregnation. It will presently be seen that anthropological and folkloristic material provides ample confirmation of these expectations.

The supposed action of salt in favoring fecundity and in preventing barrenness has been mentioned above. It was a classical belief that mice became impregnated through eating salt;[88] any objection to our hypothesis, therefore, that the connection between the ideas of salt and semen is too remote for them ever to have been brought together, except artificially, at once falls to the ground, for here we have a direct identification of the two substances. In the Pyrenees, the wedding couple before setting out for church put salt into their left pocket to guard against the man's being impotent. In Limousin, Poitou, and Haut-Vienne, the bridegroom alone does this; in Altmark, the bride alone. In Pamproux, salt is put into the

88. Pliny, *Nat. Hist.* 10.85.

clothes of the wedding couple with the same motive.[89] In Germany, salt is strewn in the bride's shoe.[90] In Scotland, on the night before the wedding, salt is strewn on the floor of the new home with the object of protecting the young couple against the evil eye;[91] I have elsewhere shown that the idea of maleficium, with which that of the evil eye is practically identical, mainly arises from the pervading dread of impotence,[92] and Seligmann actually mentions the use of salt to counteract the "ligature," i.e., the spell cast over the sexual functions by evil influences.[93]

Frobenius relates a folkloristic story told with the directness of peasant thought.[94] A penis and vagina once went together on a journey to buy salt. Each carried its portion. On the way back it began to rain. The vagina said to her comrade: "Our salt will get wet if we carry it on our heads. Let us put it in my opening; then it will keep dry." They did this, and there we have the reason why the penis ever seeks the vagina since it contains the daintiest delicacy (i.e., salt), while the vagina always wants salt (i.e., semen) from the penis.

Salt has often, especially in former times, been considered to have an exciting influence on the nervous system, and it was thus thought to possess the attribute of arousing passion and desire.[95] Schleiden writes: "The Romans termed a man in love 'salax' (whence our 'salacious'), and this view still survives with us when we jokingly say that the cook who has put too much salt into the soup must be in love."[96] In Belgium the custom of visiting one's sweetheart in the nights after festivals is called

---

89. The preceding examples are all taken from Seligmann, *Der böse Blick und Verwandtes,* 2: 35–36, and Schleiden, *Das Salz,* 71, 79.

90. Otto Schell, "Das Salz im Volksglauben," *Zeitschrift des Vereins für Volkskunde* 15 (1905): 146.

91. Seligmann, *Der böse Blick,* 2: 35.

92. Ernest Jones, *Der Alptraum in seiner Beziehung zu gewissen Formen des mittelalterlichen Aberglaubens,* translated by E. H. Sachs (Leipzig and Vienna: Franz Deuticke, 1912), 107–8.

93. Seligmann, *Der böse Blick,* 2: 291.

94. Leo Frobenius, *Schwarze Seelen: Afrikanisches Tag- und Nachtleben* (Berlin-Charlottenburg: Vita, Deutsches Verlagshaus, 1913), 433.

95. Schleiden, *Das Salz,* 92.

96. Ibid., 93.

"turning one's love into salt."[97] Shakespeare evidently uses it in the same sense in the passage "Though we are justices...we have some salt of our youth in us."[98] In some stories collected among African natives by Frobenius[99] salt is referred to as a direct equivalent of semen. Paracelsus, in his *De Origine Morborum Invisibilium*,[100] teaches that Incubi and Succubi emanate from the sperma found in the imagination of those who commit the unnatural sin of Onan, but that this is no true sperma, only corrupted salt.

The following are two metaphorical applications of the same idea. Salt is used to keep the fire always burning,[101] and there are examples, which need not be quoted, of the combination of salt and fire being used for every purpose in regard to which salt alone has superstitiously been used. At the Osiris festivals in Egypt all those taking part had to light lamps the oil of which had had salt mixed with it.[102] The idea of fire, however, in poetry as well as in mythology,[103] is constantly used to represent the ideas of the fire of life and the fire of love. Again, lameness is often brought into symbolic association with impotence (incapacity, inability), and in Sicily salt is used specifically to prevent lameness.[104]

The initiatory ceremonies universally performed by ruder peoples at the age of puberty commonly include a sacrificial or propitiatory act; circumcision is a replacement of such ceremonies, having been put back to the age of infancy just as baptism has been by most Christian Churches. In Egypt, salt is strewn when circumcision is performed.[105]

---

97. "Volksgebräuche in den Kempen," in Ida von Düringsfeld and Otto Freiherr von Reinsberg-Düringsfeld, *Ethnographische Curiositäten* (Leipzig: Alfred Krüger, 1879), 2. Abt., 135.

98. William Shakespeare, *The Merry Wives of Windsor*, Act 2, Sc. 3.

99. Frobenius, *Schwarze Seelen*, 433. Dr. Otto Rank kindly informed me of this.

100. Hartmann, *Life of Paracelsus*, 90.

101. Elard Mühlhause, *Urreligion des deutschen Volkes in hessischen Sitten, Sagen, Redensarten, Sprichwörtern und Namen* (Kassel: Theodor Fischer, 1860), 133.

102. Schleiden, *Das Salz*, 76.

103. Karl Abraham, *Traum und Mythus: Eine Studie zur Völkerpsychologie* (Leipzig and Vienna: Franz Deuticke, 1909).

104. Pitré, *Usi e costumi*, 3: 426.

105. Seligmann, *Der böse Blick*, 2: 37.

In various initiations, both earnest and jocular, at universities and schools salt played a central part, and the phrase "to salt a freshman" is still in vogue.[106] Of late years it has been replaced in this respect by the more convenient alcohol, another unconscious symbol for semen,[107] but the feeling-attitude remains the same-namely, that the young man needs the administration of an essential substance before he can be regarded as having attained full virility.

It is known that there exists an intimate connection between extreme *abstinence* attitudes of all kinds and excessive sexual "repression;" over-great prudishness is apt to be accompanied by a desire to abolish all alcohol from the universe, as we see at the present day in America. In the same way salt has been brought into manifold relation with the idea of sexual abstinence. The workers in the salt-pans near Siphoum, in Laos, must abstain from all sexual relations at the place where they are at work, the motive being a purely superstitious one.[108] The celibate Egyptian priests had at certain times to abstain wholly from the use of salt, on the ground of its being a material that excited sensual desires too much. [109] Abstinence both from sexual relations and from the partaking of salt is enjoined for several days on men of the Dyak tribes after returning from an expedition in which they have taken human heads,[110] and for three weeks on a Pima Indian who has killed an Apache; [111] in the latter case the man's wife also has to abstain from salt during the same period.[112]

---

106. Cf. Brand, *Observations on the Popular Antiquities*, 1 : 433–39.

107. "Die psychologischen Beziehungen zwischen Sexualität und Alkoholismus," in Karl Abraham, *Klinische Beiträge zur Psychoanalyse aus den Jahren 1907–1920* (Leipzig, Vienna, and Zurich: Internationaler Pyschoanalytischer Verlag, 1921): 40f.

108. Étienne Aymonier, *Notes sur le Laos* (Saigon: Imprimerie du Gouvernement, 1885), 141.

109. Schleiden, *Das Salz*, 93.

110. S.W. Tromp, "Uit de Salasila van Koetei," *Bijdragen tot de Taal-, Land-, en Volkenkunde van Nederlandsch-Indië* 37, no. 1 (1888): 74.

111. Hubert Howe Bancroft, *The Native Races of the Pacific States*, 5 vols. (New York: D. Appleton and Company, 1875–76), 1 : 553; J.W. Powell, *Ninth Annual Report of the Bureau of Ethnology to the Secretary of the Smithsonian Institution 1887–88* (Washington: Government Printing Office, 1892), 475.

112. Frank Russell, "The Pima Indians," in *Twenty-Sixth Annual Report of the Bureau of American Ethnology to the Secretary of the Smithsonian Institution 1904–1905*

The full account of these customs clearly shows that they constitute rites of purification and expiation. Abstinence both from sexual relations and from salt is also frequently prescribed during important undertakings or on weighty occasions: thus on Lake Victoria Nyanza while fishing,[113] and in the island of Nias while traps are being laid for wild animals.[114] In Uganda any man who has either committed adultery or eaten salt is not allowed to partake of the sacred fishoffering.[115] In Mexico, the Huichol Indians undergo the same double abstinence while the sacred cactus plant, the gourd of the God of Fire, is being gathered.[116] Similar double observances obtain in other countries in connection with the promotion of fertility; in fact the last-named custom is related to this, for the main benefits that the sacred cactus is supposed to bestow are plentiful rain supply, good crops, and the like. The Indians of Peru abstain for as long as six months both from sexual intercourse and from eating salt on the occasion of the birth of twins; one of the twins was believed to be the son of the lightning, the lord and creator of rain.[117] Other examples of the same double abstinence are: in Peru, preceding the Acatay mita festival, the object of which is to ripen the fruit, and which is followed by a sexual orgy;[118] in Nicaragua, from the time that the maize is sown until it is reaped.[119] In Behar, India, the Nagin women, sacred prostitutes known as "wives of the Snake-God," periodically go about begging and

---

(Washington: Government Printing Office, 1908), 204.

113. Sir James George Frazer, *The Golden Bough: A Study in Magic and Religion*, Part II: *Taboo and the Perils of the Soul* (London: Macmillan and Co., 1911), 194.

114. J.W. Thomas, "De jacht op het eiland Nias," *Tijdschrift voor Indische Taal-, Land-, en Volkenkunde* 26 (1881): 276.

115. J. Roscoe, "Further Notes on the Manners and Customs of the Baganda," *The Journal of the Royal Anthropological Institute of Great Britain and Ireland* 32 (January–June 1902): 56.

116. Carl Lumholtz, *Unknown Mexico: A Record of Five Years's Exploration Among the Tribes of the Western Sierra Madre; in the Tierra Caliente of Tepec and Jalisco; and Among the Tarascos of Michoacan*, 2 vols (New York: Charles Scribner's Sons, 1902–3), 2: 126.

117. Sir James George Frazer, *The Golden Bough: A Study in Magic and Religion*, Part I: *The Magic Art and the Evolution of Kings*, 2 vols. (London: Macmillan and Co., 1911), 1: 266.

118. Frazer, *Taboo and the Perils of the Soul*, 98.

119. Frazer, *The Magic Art*, 2: 105.

during this time they may not touch salt; half of their proceeds go to the priests and half to buying salt and sweetmeats for the villagers.[120] Attention may be called to two features of the preceding collection of customs. First, that they occur in all parts of the globe, instances having been cited from Europe, Africa, Asia, and America, North, South, and Central. Secondly, that to a great extent they duplicate the customs previously described in connection with salt alone, thus in relation to religion, to the weather, to important undertakings, and to the production of fertility. Where in one country the presence of salt is indispensable, in another one abstinence from salt—and at the same time from sexual intercourse—is equally essential. Both cases agree in regarding salt as an important agent in these respects; whether this is for good or for evil is of secondary interest, the main point being its significance. If, as is here suggested, the idea of salt is generally connected in the unconscious mind with that of semen, it is throughout intelligible that abstinence from sexual relations should tend to be accompanied by abstinence from salt as well (radiation of the affect); it is in perfect accord with all we know of primitive, symbolic thinking. The unconscious logic of the argument seems to be that abstinence from sexuality is incomplete unless all forms of semen, even symbolic forms, are abstained from.

This bipolar attitude of regarding salt as either exceedingly beneficial or exceedingly harmful reminds one of two current controversies—namely, whether alcohol and sexual intercourse respectively are beneficial or harmful to health. Indeed, as with these, there have been at various times propagandist movements started in which salt has been denounced as the cause of numerous bodily evils.[121] In 1851 there was published a volume by a Dr. Robert Howard entitled *Salt, the Forbidden Fruit or Food*.[122] It was described by the *Lancet* as "worthy of immortality." As

---

120. W. Crooke, *The Popular Religion and Folk-Lore of Northern India,* 2 vols. (Westminster: Archibald Constable & Co., 1896), 2: 138.

121. Lawrence, *The Magic of the Horse-Shoe,* 189–90.

122. Robert Howard, *Salt, the Forbidden Fruit or Food; and the Chief Causes of Diseases of the Body and Mind of Man, and of Animals; As Taught by the Ancient Egyptian Priests and Wise Men, and by Scripture; in Accordance with the Author's Experience of Many Years* (London: Piper, Brothers, & Co., 1851).

may be imagined from the title, the author treats of salt as a most obnoxious substance, abstinence from which is essential to the maintenance of health. It is possible even that unconscious associations of the kind under consideration may not have been altogether without influence in relation to more recent medical views. It had long been noticed that urine contained solid constituents which were either evident as such or could be recovered from their soluble state by means of evaporation; these were regarded on the one hand as comprising the essence of the fluid, being thus identified with semen, and on the other as salts, which indeed they mostly are.[123] The sufferings due to the excessive accumulation of these salts, in the form of calculi, attracted a great deal of attention and play a very important part in early surgical writings. When the chemical constituents of urine came to be carefully studied by exact methods there arose a tendency, which reached its acme in the late 1880s, to attribute a considerable number of disorders to the presence in the system of an excessive amount of these constituents. Thus, to mention only a few examples, gout was thought to be simply a question of poisoning by uric acid, uremia to be poisoning with urea, diabetic coma (exhaustion following on the continued loss of a vital substance), poisoning by acetone (an occasional urinary constituent), rheumatism poisoning by lactic acid (milk, a sexual secretion, is almost constantly identified with semen in the unconscious), and so on. It is interesting that the two diseases in regard to which this idea was most firmly fixed—namely, gout and rheumatism—are joint diseases, and hence lend themselves to the series of unconscious associations "lameness-incapacity-impotence." Of late years the tendency has taken at the same time simpler and more complex directions. On the one hand there is a return to salt itself, and a "salt-free diet" is vaunted as the sovereign agent for the prevention of arterial disease and old age (impotency), for the cure of epilepsy, and so on. It will also be remembered how, when Brown-Séquard's attempt to recapture youthful vigor by means of the injection of canine semen shocked the medical profession in London, efforts were made to substitute the more respectable, because unconscious, symbol of this—common salt. On the

123. The unconscious association between semen and urine on the one hand and salt and water on the other will be dealt with at length later in this essay.

other hand there is a restless search for more complex organic poisons, usually in the intestinal contents, which are now being as extensively exploited as the urine was forty years ago. The belief in the prime importance of organic poisons is even generally extended to psychosexual maladies, such as hysteria, "neurasthenia," and dementia praecox. It may be questioned whether the important advance in knowledge represented by the toxic theory of disease would not have met with more resistance than it did had it not appealed to a fundamental complex in the human mind, in which, among others, the ideas of poison and semen are closely associated.

The *salt-cellar,* the receptacle of the salt, has been held in as much superstitious reverence as its contents.[124] The symbolism of it is usually a feminine one,[125] as indeed is indicated by the Spanish compliment of calling a sweetheart "salt-cellar of my love."[126] Salt-cellars, often of great magnificence, were, and still are, favorite wedding-presents. In Rome they constituted a special heirloom, the *paternum salinum,* which was handed down from generation to generation with especial care. In general it is just as evident that an excessive amount of affect, of extraneous origin, has been invested in the idea of a salt-cellar as it is in salt itself. In classical times the salt-cellar partook of the nature of a holy vessel, associated with the temple in general, and more particularly with the altar.[127] To those who are familiar with the female symbolism of the altar[128] this will be quite comprehensible. The etymology of the word "salt-cellar" is of considerable interest in the present connection. The second part, "cellar," is derived from the French *salière* (salt-cellar), so that the whole is a redundancy, meaning "salt-salt-receptacle." We see here an instructive example of linguistic assimilation, for a "cellar" (a dark chamber

124. Schleiden, *Das Salz,* 74; Lawrence, *The Magic of the Horse-Shoe,* 196–205.

125. Though the late Dr. Putnam related to me the case of a man in whose dreams a salt-cellar appeared as a symbol of the scrotum.

126. Karl Andree, "Sevilla und das Volksleben in Andalusien," *Globus: Illustrierte Zeitschrift für Länder- und Völkerkunde* 11 (1867): 140.

127. Schleiden, *Das Salz,* 74.

128. George W. Cox, *The Mythology of the Aryan Nations,* 2 vols. (London: Longmans, Green, and Co., 1870), 2: 113–21; Thomas Inman, *Ancient Pagan and Modern Christian Symbolism* (New York: Peter Eckler Publishing Company, 1922), 74.

under the house) has the same feminine symbolic meaning as *salière* itself. The sound resemblance of the words *salière* and cellar naturally made the assimilation easier, but the instinctive intuition of the people was probably the underlying factor in bringing it about.

The offering of salt as a special mark of favor, and as a sign of hospitality, has been mentioned above; we have now to note the reverse of this. In England[129] and France,[130] it was considered unlucky to be helped to salt at table; this superstition still obtains in Anglican circles and finds popular expression in the saying "Help me to salt, help me to sorrow." In Russia, the quarrel that would otherwise follow can be averted if one smiles amicably when proffering the salt.[131]

III.

In the preceding section of this essay we dealt chiefly with the *adult* roots of salt symbolism and superstitions, and we have now to turn our attention to the deeper *infantile* roots. The reason why the word "deeper" is used here will presently become evident; it has to do with the ontogenetic, as well as phylogenetic, antiquity of symbolism in general.

Before passing to the next stage of the investigation, therefore, it will be necessary briefly to refer to some aspects of infantile mental life that without being realized play an important part in adult life—namely, certain views developed by young children concerning the begetting of children.[132] These are forgotten long before puberty, so that the adult is quite unaware of their existence and is extremely surprised to hear of their great frequency in childhood life. They survive nevertheless in the unconscious mind, and exert a considerable influence on later interests and views.

---

129. Brand, *Observations on the Popular Antiquities*, 3: 162

130. Ibid., 3: 163.

131. Jean Fleury, "Superstitions russes," *Revue des Traditions populaires* 1, no. 5 (25 May 1886): 149; Sikes, *British Goblins*, 329.

132. See "Über infantile Sexualtheorien," in Sigmund Freud, *Sammlung kleiner Schriften zur Neurosenlehre*, Zweite Folge (Leipzig and Vienna: Franz Deuticke, 1911), 159–64,

Early realizing, in spite of the untruths told him by the parents, that a baby is born of the mother and grows inside her, the child sets to work to solve the problem as best he can, the full answer being concealed from him. Knowing nothing of other organs he conceives of the "inside," particularly the abdomen, as simply a receptacle for food, a view amply confirmed by his experience of indigestion and other sensations. The baby, therefore, must have been formed out of food, an inference that is largely correct. Further, there being no other mode of exit possible—at least so far as he is aware—the baby must have then reached the exterior in the same way as digested food (cloaca theory), as it actually does in all animals except mammalia. There is thus established in the child's mind a close connection between the ideas of food, feces, and babies, one that explains among many other things many an hysterical symptom in later life.

The child next comes to the notion that, since food alone does not in his personal experience have this result, a mixing of two substances must be necessary. On the basis of his excremental interests he observes that there are three possible materials available, for it is only exceptionally that he thinks the fertilizing material is of nonhuman origin. The fantasy may combine these three materials—solid, liquid, and gaseous—in different ways, the commonest of which, in my experience and in that of other observers, are in order: liquid-solid, liquid-liquid, solid-solid, and gaseous-solid. A knowledge of these facts is indispensable for the full understanding of salt symbolism. As the objection may be raised that they are artifacts of the psychoanalytic method of investigation, it will be well to refer to a little of the mass of purely anthropological evidence that proves the universal occurrence of similar beliefs in what corresponds with the childhood of the race.[133]

The belief that fertilization, and even delivery, can take place through some other orifice than the vagina has been held in the most diverse countries of the world and is still quite prevalent. Any orifice or

---

133. Since this essay was written a highly interesting paper of Otto Rank's has appeared in which a large quantity of additional data is given that both confirms and amplifies the conclusions here enunciated ("Völkerpsychologische Parallelen zu den infantilen Sexualtheorien," *Zentralblatt for Psychoanalyse* 2, no. 8 [1912]: 425–37).

indentation may be implicated, the nostril, eye, ear, navel, and so on. An interesting historical example was the medieval belief that the Virgin Mary conceived through the ear, one widely held in the Roman Catholic Church.[134] The mouth, however, was the orifice most frequently thought of in this connection, as is apparent from the very numerous legends and beliefs in which eating or drinking bring about pregnancy. The peasantry in England still believe that peahens are impregnated in this way,[135] and similar views are entertained in other countries in respect of different animals.

A digression must here be made on a matter of some importance to the present theme—namely, the association between food as taken into the body and food as it is given out, two ideas which are by no means so remote from each other in the primitive mind, including that of the child, as they usually are in that of the civilized adult. In the first place many savage tribes have the custom of devouring ordure of all kinds, including their own, and indeed seem to partake of it with special relish;[136] a contemptuous reference to it may be found in 2 Kings 18: 27. In more civilized countries this has long been replaced by sausages[137] (a word, by the way, of the same etymological derivation as salt), and other products of abdominal organs.[138] The ordure of sacred men has in many countries, e.g., Tibet, a high religious significance, being used to anoint kings, to guard against evil demons, and so on.[139] That it is not very rare for

134. See Chapter 13 of my *Essays in Applied Psychoanalysis,* vol. 2, which is devoted to an examination of this belief ("The Madonna's Conception through the Ear").

135. Edwin Sidney Hartland, *Primitive Paternity: The myth of Supernatural Birth in Relation to the History of the Family,* 2 vols. (London: David Nutt, 1909–10), 1: 51.

136. Captain John G. Bourke, *Scatalogic Rites of All Nations* (Washngton, D.C.: W.H. Lowdermilk & Co., 1891), 33–37.

137. In English, in the present generation, the belief was acted on that a stolen sausage had the power of curing barrenness (Hartland, *Primitive Paternity,* 1 : 56).

138. The wife of the Elector of Hanover, in a letter to her niece, the sister-in-law of Louis XIV, writes: "Si la viande fait la merde, il est vrai de dire que la merde fait la viande. Est-ce que clans les tables les plus delicates, la merde n'y est pas servie en ragouts?... Les boudins, les andouilles, les saucisses, no sont-ce pas de ragouts clans des sacs a merde?," 31 Octobre 1694, in *Correspondenance complète de Madame Duchesse d'Orléans,* vol. 1 (Paris: Bibliotheque-Charpentier, 1891), n.p.

139. Bourke, *Scatalogic Rites,* 42–53.

insane patients to eat their own excrement is of course well-known;[140] in such cases the long-buried infantile association may come to open expression in the patient's remark, pointing to the excrement, that he has just produced a baby. Cases of stercophagy are occasionally met with apart from any psychosis, as I know from personal experience of several instances. An association is often formed between the ideas of excrement and corpses, probably through the common notion of decomposition of something that was once a living human body, or part of one. Both ideas are connected with that of fecundity.

Mainly derived from the same source are the beliefs and customs relating to the endless magical properties attaching to dead bodies, and notably to their most putrefactive elements (saliva, excretions, etc.).[141] It would be out of place to follow this subject further here.

A more constant unconscious association is that between the ideas of *gold* and *feces*,[142] one of far-reaching significance in mythology as well as in the reactions of everyday life. Gold as fertilizing principle usually in conjunction with a second sexual symbol is a favorite theme in mythology; perhaps the best known instance is that of Dame being impregnated by a shower of golden rain. Apples, fish, and other objects, made of or resembling gold, are also familiar instances of the same type of story. This association explains the extensive connection noted earlier between salt and money or wealth (both being symbols of fertilizing excrement).

Pregnancy has been brought about just as frequently by drinking as it has by eating; all manner of fluids have been efficacious in this respect, the sacred soma-juice milk, the sap of grass, leaves and plants, the juice of roots, fruit and flowers, and so on.[143] The idea of a *liquid* stimulus to conception thus stands in contrast with that of a solid one. The practice

---

140. According to Heinrich Obersteiner, this is true of one percent of such patients, more often with men.

141. Edwin Sidney Hartland, *The Legend of Perseus: A Study in Story Custom and Belief,* vol. 2: *The Life Token* (London: David Nutt, 1895), 162–74, 313–32.

142. "Charakter und Analerotik," in Freud, *Sammlung kleiner Schriften zur Neurosenlehre,* 136–37; "The Ontogenesis of the Interest in Money," in Sándor Ferenczi, *Contributions to Psycho-Analysis* (Boston: Richard G. Badger, 1916), 269–79; "The Anal-Erotic Character Traits," in Jones, *Papers on Psycho-Analysis,* 676–88.

143. Hartland, *Primitive Paternity,* vol. 1 (numerous instances).

of drinking various fluids for the purpose of aiding conception is even more widely spread, and exists throughout Europe at the present day. In every country women wishing to have children drink water from various holy springs or wells, the most potent of which is perhaps that at Lourdes.[144] Apart from this numerous allied practices exist, of which the following selection may be given. In Thuringia and Transylvania, women who wished to be healed of unfruitfulness drank consecrated (salt) water from the baptismal font.[145]

As might be expected, more personal fluids are extensively used for the same purpose, this being the primary sense of the proceeding. In Bombay, a woman cuts off the end of the robe of another woman who has borne children, steeps it, and drinks the infusion. Other women in India drink the water squeezed from the loincloth of a sanyasi or devotee. Saliva has been very extensively employed in this connection, it being almost universally treated as a seminal equivalent (hence the expression "he is the very spit of his father"). Saliva in fact forms throughout in folklore and superstition a regular duplicate of salt, bearing the same relation to hospitality, friendship, compacts, baptism, magical powers and charms, religious significance, and the rest;[146] the theme cannot be further pursued here and obviously needs separate exposition. Other fluids that may be mentioned are: the milk of another woman, blood from the navel of a new-born child, water in which the navel has been soaked, the lochial discharge of a woman at her first child-bed, water in which the placenta has been soaked, water from the first bath of a woman after delivery. The original sense of all these beliefs and customs is revealed by consideration of the numerous myths and legends, which recur in every part of the world without exception, describing how pregnancy followed the imbibing of semen, deliberate or accidental.

A great part of our mental life, however, is the echo of childhood thoughts, and the child knows nothing about semen. To him the corresponding potent fluid is *urine*, a topic which must next concern us. The prediction was ventured above that the various ideas noted in regard to

---

144. Ibid., 64–67.
145. Ibid., 67.
146. Hartland, *The Legend of Perseus*, 258–75.

salt and water would be found to mirror earlier corresponding ones relating to semen and urine. Confining ourselves for the present to the subject of salt water and urine, we find that the resemblances between the ideas relating to them are very striking. They may be considered by following the order in which the properties of salt were enumerated at the outset.

The significance of salt for friendship, loyalty, hospitality, and the ratifying of pacts, was dwelt on above: the same customs and ideas can be duplicated in respect to urine. Until about three centuries ago it was the vogue in Europe to pledge a friend's health in urine,[147] exactly as we now do in wine, and in the same circumstances; by this, perpetual friendship and loyalty, or even love attachment, might be ensured. The same custom still obtains in Siberia, where it also signifies a pact of peace.[148] At a Moorish wedding the bride's urine is thrown in the face of any unmarried man or stranger on whom it is wished to bestow a distinguished favor,[149] just as in other countries salt is presented with the same intention.

The magical powers of salt are fully equalled by those of urine. In connection with evil spirits and witches it played a triple part. In the first place it was used actually to bewitch people for evil purposes.[150]

It may be added that sometimes we find salt combined with urine for medical purposes, e.g., to get rid of a fever.[151]

The importance of salt for fecundity is if anything exceeded by that of urine. It formed the essential constituent of many love-philtres and magical procedures having as their object the winning of affection.[152]

---

147. Bourke, *Scatalogic Rites*, 129. Numerous references. ("Cobblers' punch means urine with a cinder in it.")

148. George W. Melville, *In the Lena Delta: A Narrative of the Search for Lieut.-Commander DeLong and His Companions, Followed by an Account of the Greely Relief Expedition and a Proposed Method of Reaching the North Pole* (Boston: Houghton, Mifflin and Company, 1885), 318.

149. Mungo Park, *Travels, in the Interior Districts of Africa: Performed under the Direction and Patronage of the African Association in the Years 1795, 1796, and 1797* (New York: Evert Duyckinck, 1813), 109, 135.

150. Johann Christian Frommann, *Tractatus de fascinatione novus et singularis* (Nuremberg: Wolfgang Moritz Endter und Johann Andreas Endter, 1674), 683.

151. Wuttke, *Der deutsche Volksaberglaube*, 354.

152. Bourke, *Scatalogic Rites*, 216–17, 223.

The use of salt at initiation ceremonies can also be paralleled with that of urine. A young Parsee undergoes a kind of confirmation during which he is made to drink a small quantity of the urine of a bull.[153] At the Hottentot initiation ceremony one of the medicine men urinates over the youth, who proudly rubs the fluid into his skin.[154] Corresponding with the Christian and Jewish displacement of their initiation ceremonies (baptism, circumcision) from the time of puberty to that of infancy we find a similar displacement in respect of urine ceremonies. The Californian Indians give their children a draught of urine as soon as they are born,[155] and this custom is also in vogue amongst Americans in the country districts;[156] these are of course not pure examples of initiation. The Injit child selected to be trained as an Angekok was bathed in urine soon after birth as a religious ceremony.[157] When Parsee children are invested with the Sudrâ and Kusti—the badges of the Zoroastrian faith—they are sprinkled with the urine of a sacred cow and they also have to drink some of it.[158]

The interest aroused by the taste of salt may be compared with that taken in the peculiar taste of urine, a matter that played a considerable part in medical urinoscopy. All bodily fluids, including tears, semen, sweat, blood, etc., owe of course most of their taste to the presence of salt in them. The natives of Northern Siberia habitually drink each other's urine.[159] The African Shillooks regularly wash out their milk vessels

---

153. Monier Williams, *Modern India and the Indians: Being a Series of Impressions, Notes, and Essays* (London: Trübner and Co., 1878), 178.

154. "The Voyages of Peter Kolben, A.M. to the Cape of God Hope," in *A New Collection of Voyages, Discoveries and Travels: Containing Whatever Is Worthy of Notice, in Europe, Asia, Africa, and America*, vol. 2 (London: J. Knox, 1767), 399–400; "Thunberg's Account of the Cape of God Hope," in John Pinkerton, *A General Collection of the Best and Most Interesting Voyages and Travels in All Parts of the World*, vol. 16 (London: Longman, Hurst, Rees, Orme, and Brown, 1814), 89, 141.

155. Bancroft, *The Native Races of the Pacific States*, 1: 413.

156. Trumbull, quoted by Bourke, *Scatalogic Rites*, 240.

157. Élie Réclus, *Les Primitifs: Études d'ethnologie comparée* (Paris: G. Chamerot, 1885), 84.

158. F. Max Müller, *Chips from a German Workshop*, vol. 1: *Essays on the Science of Religion* (New York: Charles Scribner and Company, 1872), 63–64.

159. Melville, quoted by Bourke, *Scatalogic Rites*, 38.

with urine "probably," so Schweinfurth[160] thinks, "to compensate for a lack of salt;" this is also done by the natives of Eastern Siberia.[161] The Obbe[162] and other natives[163] of Central Africa never drink milk unless it is mixed with urine, the reason given being that otherwise the cow would lose her milk; we have here a counterpart of the custom of mixing salt with the milk so as to ensure a plentiful supply. "Chinook olives" are acorns that have been steeped for five months in human urine.[164] Of interest is the relation of urine to the manufacture of intoxicating drinks, it being thus an equivalent to alcohol, as we have noted above. When the supply of alcohol runs short in Siberia the natives eke it out by making a mixture of equal parts of urine and alcohol.[165]

We have next to note the analogies between the significance of salt and that of urine in regard to religious performances. In both cases the substance might be either swallowed or applied to the surface of the body, and concerning the latter practice it is expedient to make a few preliminary remarks. The religious practice of sprinkling or baptizing with a holy fluid (salt and water in the Roman Catholic Church, plain water in the Protestant Church) has evidently two principal meanings. In the first place it symbolizes purification, particularly from sin. Probably the simplest and most accurate expression for the psychological meaning of baptism, as perhaps for that of any religious rite, is "purification through rebirth." The earthly incestuous libido, which is now known to be the deepest source of the sense of sin in general,[166] is overcome and purified

---

160. Georg Schweinfurth, *The Heart of Africa: Three Years' Travels and Adventures in the Unexplored Regions of Central Africa from 1868 to 1872,* translated by Ellen E. Frewer, 2 vols. (London: Sampson Low, Marston, Searle, & Rivington, 1878), 1 : 16.

161. Melville, quoted by Bourke, *Scatalogic Rites,* 200.

162. Sir Samuel W. Baker, *The Albert N'yanza Great Basin of the Nile, and Explorations of the Nile Sources* (Philadelphia: J. B. Lippincott and Co., 1869), 240.

163. Col. C. Chaillé Long, *Central Africa: Naked Truths of Naked People* (New York: Harper & Brothers, 1877), 70.

164. Paul Kane, *Wanderings of an Artist among the Indians of North America from Canada to Vancouver's Island and Oregon through the Hudson's Bay Company's Territory and Back Again* (London: Longman, Brown, Green, Longmans, and Roberts, 1859), 187.

165. Melville, quoted by Bourke, *Scatalogic Rites,* 39.

166. Sigmund Freud, *Totem und Tabu: Einige Übereinstimmungen im Seelenleben der Wilden und der Neurotiker* (Leipzig and Vienna: Hugo Heller, 1913), 144–45.

in a homeopathic manner by passing through a symbolic act of heavenly incest. Purification by fire is a distorted form of the more original purification by water. It will be noticed that in baptism the liquid symbolizes both the father's urine (or semen) and the mother's uterine waters, satisfying thus both the male and the female components of the libido. The oldest association between the ideas of liquid and purification is of course the child's experience of urine washing away feces, thus cleansing dirt (the deepest source for the objectionableness of sexuality).[167]

In the second place baptism imbues the participant with the mystic properties conveyed by, or belonging to, the holy fluid. This meaning, which was probably the original one of the two, is well illustrated in the Hottentot rite described above, where the participant scratches his skin so as to absorb as much as possible of the precious fluid. At all events we find that the acts of ablution[168] and of swallowing are throughout treated as though they were identical. Where one is performed in one country the other is in another country in exactly corresponding circumstances, and in numberless instances the two are regarded as equivalent. For example, the practice of imbibing water, particularly holy water, for the cure of barrenness, as described above, is throughout paralleled by the equally common one of bathing in water for the same purpose, and often at the same place; Hartland has collected an enormous number of instances of this from every part of the world and shows that it is today as frequent as ever.[169]

All the evidence, from comparative religions, from history, anthropology and folklore, converges to the *conclusion, not only that Christian and other rites of baptism symbolize the bestowment of a vital fluid (semen or urine) on the initiate, but that the holy water there used is a lineal descendant of urine, the use of which it gradually displaced.* Strange as this conclusion may

---

167. Sigmund Freud, "Über die allgemeine Erniedrigung des Liebeslebens," in *Jahrbuch für Psychoanalytische und Psychopathologische Forschungen*, vol. 4, edited by Eugen Bleuler, Sigmund Freud, and C. G. Jung (Leipzig and Vienna: Franz Deuticke, 1912), 49–50.

168. It should not be forgotten that the original form of Christian baptism was complete immersion; the relatively modern custom of christening, or sprinkling, is a later replacement of this, and is still repudiated by, for instance, in Baptist sects.

169. Hartland, *Primitive Paternity*, 1 : 77–89.

seem it is definitely supported by the following facts selected from a vast number of similar ones.

To begin with, it is known that salt and water has historically replaced urine in various non-religious or semi-religious usages. Bourke writes: "We shall have occasion to show that salt and water, holy water, and other liquids superseded human urine in several localities, Scotland included."[170]

In the early days of Christianity the Manichaean sect used to bathe in urine. It is related of an Irish king, Aedh, that he obtained some urine of the chief priest, bathed his face in it, drank some with gusto, and said that he prized it more highly than the Eucharist itself.[171]

In modern religions of civilized peoples, however, human urine is never used, having been replaced by water, salt and water, or cow's urine. The sacred drink hum of the Parsees has the "urine of a young, pure cow" as one of the ingredients.[172] In the Bareshnun ceremony the Parsee priest has to undergo certain ablutions wherein he applies to his body cow's urine,[173] and to rub the *nirang* (cow's urine) over his face and hands is the second thing every Parsee does after rising in the morning.[174] The latter ceremony is by no means a simple one; for instance, he is not allowed to touch anything directly with his hands until the sacred nirang has first been washed off with water. In India the urine of a cow is a holy water of the very highest religious significance. It is used in ceremonies of purification, during which it is drunk.[175] Dubois says that a Hindu penitent "must drink the *panchakaryam-a* word which literally signifies the five things, namely, milk, butter, curd, dung, and urine, all mixed together," and he adds: "The urine of a cow is held to be the most efficacious of any for purifying all imaginable uncleanness."[176]

---

170. Bourke, *Scatalogic Rites,* 211.

171. Bourke, *Scatalogic Rites,* 58–59.

172. F. Max Müller, *Biographies of Words and the Home of the Aryas* (London: Longmans, Green, and Co., 1888), 237.

173. Kingsley, quoted by Bourke, *Scatalogic Rites,* 211.

174. Müller, *Chips from a German Workshop,* 163.

175. Angelo de Gubernatis, *Zoological Mythology, or The Legends of Animals,* 2 vols. (London: Trübner & Co., 1872), 1: 95.

176. Abbé J. A. Dubois, *Description of the Character, Manners, and Customs of the People*

The interest in the combination of salt and water has naturally been extended to the sea, which has always played an important part in the birth fancies of mankind. The association is evident in the use of the Greek word *háls* (Lat. *sale*) to express both "salt" and "sea." The contrast between fire and water has often been seized upon to represent the contrast between male and female elements respectively. The relation between salt and fire is much more extensive than we have here described; most of the customs and beliefs mentioned above could be paralleled by similar ones in which it is necessary to throw salt into the fire in order to produce the desired effect.[177] In mythology, the combination of fire and water (male and female elements) is symbolized with especial frequency by alcohol, which presumably was the essential constituent of the various sacred drinks of which we read; with singular appropriateness the North American Indians refer to alcoholic beverages as "fire-water."

The association between the ideas fire-salt-sea are well shown in the following myths. From the mythical lore of Finland we learn that Ukko, the mighty god of the sky, struck fire in the heavens; a spark descended from this was received by the waves and became salt.[178] This example is especially instructive for more than one reason. In the first place we here have salt directly derived from fire, thus confirming our previous surmise of the symbolic equivalency of the two. In the next place, as Abraham[179] has clearly demonstrated, heavenly fire descending upon earth, e.g., lightning, is mythologically only another variant of the various divine foods (soma, ambrosia, nectar) that symbolize the male fertilizing fluid; this is in obvious accord with the view here maintained of the seminal symbolism of salt.

In another myth, we have the Prometheus-like bringer of salt regarded as a Messiah. Lawrence writes: "The Chinese worship an idol called Phelo, in honor of a mythological personage of that name, whom they believe to have been the discoverer of salt and the originator of its use. His ungrateful

---

of India; and of Their Institutions, Religious and Civil (London: Longman, Hurst, Rees, Orme, and Brown, 1817), 29.

177. The etymological aspects of this relationship will be discussed later.

178. Quoted from Lawrence, *The Magic of the Horse-Shoe,* 154.

179. Abraham, "Die psychologischen Beziehungen zwischen Sexualität und Alkoholismus," 49, 62.

countrymen, however, were tardy in their recognition of Phelo's merits, and that worthy thereupon left his native land and did not return. Then the Chinese declared him to be a deity, and in the month of June each year they hold a festival in his honor, during which he is everywhere sought, but in vain; he will not appear until he comes to announce the end of the world."[180] The Prometheus theme of a god bringing an all-precious substance as a gift to mankind[181] is here worked into a form that closely resembles the Jewish conception of a Messiah that has to be sought and the Christian one of a prophet who was not received when he delivered his message, but who will return to announce the end of the world.

Tacitus refers to the belief that salt is the product of the strife between fire and water,[182] a belief evidently mirroring the infantile sadistic conception of coitus, but one that happens to have an objective basis in regard to the evaporating action of the sun's heat. On a lowlier plane we may refer to the connection between fire and water as shown by some practices carried out for the purpose of obtaining children. A Transylvanian Gypsy woman is said to drink water into which her husband has cast hot coals, or, better still, has spit, saying as she does so: "Where I am flame, be thou the coals! Where I am rain be thou the water!"[183] A South Slavonic woman holds a wooden bowl of water near the fire on the hearth. Her husband then strikes two firebrands together until the sparks fly. Some of them fall into the bowl, and she then drinks the water.[184] Of the many instances of association between the ideas of fire and urine one only need be mentioned. At the yearly ceremony held by the Eskimos for the purpose of driving out an evil spirit called Tuna, one of the performers brings a vessel of urine and flings it on the fire.[185] The ideas, therefore,

---

180. Lawrence, *The Magic of the Horse-Shoe*, 154–55.

181. See Abraham, "Die psychologischen Beziehungen zwischen Sexualität und Alkoholismus," for a full analysis of the Prometheus myth.

182. Cited by Schleiden, *Das Salz*, 11.

183. H. Ploss, *Das Weib in der Natur- und Völkerkunde*, 2 vols. (Leipzig: Th. Grieben, 1885), 2: 332.

184. Friedrich S. Krauss, *Sitte und Brauch der Südslaven nach heimischen gedruckten und ungedruckten Quellen* (Vienna: Alfred Hölder, 1885), 531.

185. *Report of the International Polar Expedition to Point Barrow, Alaska* (Washington, D.C.: Government Printing Office, 1885), 42.

of fire-salt, fire-water, and fire-urine are thus seen to be closely related in the primitive mind, a fact which stands in full harmony with the clinical psychoanalytic finding that the ideas of fire, water, urine, and semen are interchangeable equivalents in the unconscious, fire being a typical symbol for urine.

I wish here to say something about an interesting feature of superstition in general, and of salt symbolism in particular—namely, its *ambivalence*. It has often puzzled observers of superstitions to note that the very same custom or happening is supposed in one place to bring luck, in another ill luck, in the one place to lead to fertility, in another sterility, and so on. The explanation is to be found in the ambivalent attitude of consciousness to the content of the unconscious, the source of all superstitions. If the affect, which is always positive, that accompanies the unconscious idea finds a passage-way into consciousness, as happens, for instance, in the process known as sublimation, then the attitude towards the conscious representative of this idea (i.e., towards the symbol) will be correspondingly positive, and the symbolic idea will be considered the source of all good. If, on the contrary, it is the affect belonging to the "repressing" tendencies that gets attached to the symbolic idea, then the latter will come to be the sign of all that is unlucky or dangerous. The same ambivalence is seen in regard to all products of the unconscious, for instance in totemism—whether of the race or of the individual; the same animal can be loved in infancy and unreasonably feared in later childhood. So, as was remarked earlier in this essay, it is really irrelevant whether a given superstition is met with in a positive or a negative sense, the essential point being the evidence given by both of an excessive significance derived from the unconscious.

This ambivalence can be well demonstrated in salt superstitions. One finds that practically every attribute described above as being attached to the idea of salt may in other places be replaced by its exact opposite. We may illustrate this feature by selecting a few examples of contrasting pairs.

1. *Fruitfulness–Unfruitfulness*

The remarkably close association between the ideas of salt and fecundity was dwelt on in detail in the earlier part of this essay, and a few examples were also quoted in which the former idea was related to that of barrenness. This latter seems to have been more especially common in Eastern countries, and is repeatedly referred to in the Bible (e.g., Deuteronomy 29: 23; Job 39: 6; Jeremiah 17: 6; Psalms 107: 33, 34, etc.); it is also remarked on by Pliny, Virgil, and other classical writers.[186] A real ground for it was no doubt the frequent sight of salty deserts and waste places where an excess of salt had prevented all growth. This real justification for the association between salt and barrenness makes still more striking the far commoner one between it and fertility, and again shows how the latter belief must have been caused by a false association of ideas, as has been maintained above.

The analogy is again evident here between the ideas of salt, of which either the absence or the excess prevents fruitfulness, and sexuality, concerning which the same is widely believed. It is thus appropriate that Lot's wife, as a punishment for regretting the (homosexual) sins of Sodom, should have been turned into a pillar (phallus) of salt.

2. *Creation–Destruction*

This antithesis is, of course, closely allied to the last one and might also be expressed as the contrast between immortality and death. It has at all ages been a common custom to add strength to a curse by strewing salt as a symbol of destruction; historical examples are: after the destruction of Sichem by Abimelech, of Carthage by the Romans, of Padua by Attila, and of Milan by Friedrich Barbarossa. The custom seems to have had especial reference to the overpowering of a town (a mother symbol), another hint of the unconscious association between creation and destruction (compare the beliefs in the fructifying and the destroying sun).

3. *Use of Salt–Abstention from Salt*

This antithesis may be mentioned in the same connection. This has been discussed above in relation to religious observances and the question of sexual abstinence.

---

186. Schleiden, *Das Salz*, 94.

4. Value–Worthlessness

The extraordinarily high sense of value often attached to the idea of salt, and also the close relation between it and that of money or wealth, has been described above, and we have now to note the opposite of this. Schleiden, after quoting passages from Homer and Theocritus to the same effect, says: "A grain or two of salt thus became an expression for the most worthless thing that one could name. We still say, when we want to denote anything trifling: 'With that one couldn't even earn the salt for one's bread.'" [187] The same attitude of depreciation is shown in the joke of the traveler who after partaking of an extremely poor meal at an inn called the landlord to him and said: "There was one thing in this meal that I have not seen surpassed in all my travels." On the expectant landlord inquiring what it was, the traveler crushingly answered: "The salt."

5. Health–Unhealthiness

We have noted above the discussion whether the partaking of salt is especially a health-bringing procedure or the exact opposite.

6. Purity–Impurity

The Salt has always served as an emblem of immaculateness and purity. Pythagoras says in this connection: "It was begotten of the purest parents, of the sun and the sea" (another example, by the way, of the signification of fire and water that was pointed out above). The important part salt has played, e.g., in religion, in regard to purification need not again be insisted on. The extraordinarily close association between the ideas of salt and of Salt has always served as an emblem of immaculateness and purity. Pythagoras says in this connection: "It was begotten of the purest parents, of the sun and the sea" (another example, by the way, of the signification of fire and water that was pointed out above). The important part salt has played, e.g., in religion, in regard to purification need not again be insisted on. The extraordinarily close association between the ideas of salt and of the excretions, i.e., dirty processes, on the other hand, has been pointed out in detail above, and we shall presently have to note the same thing in

---

187. Schleiden, *Das Salz*, 101.

connection with the etymological history of the word. There is thus here the sharpest contrast between two opposite conceptions.

7. *Friendliness–Unfriendliness*

Whereas the offering of salt is generally a sign of friendly intentions, we have also noted examples of the exact opposite.

We have already discussed the significance of this striking ambivalence. It is a characteristic of all ideas that have deep unconscious roots, and may roughly be said to correspond with the antithesis of "the repressing" and "the repressed" as well as that between love and hate. The obverse of this statement is also true, that an idea which shows pronounced ambivalence in its affective values must have important associations in the unconscious. From the fact alone, therefore, that the idea of salt shows such marked ambivalence it could have been surmised that it has been invested with extrinsic significance of unconscious origin. One also gets here a further clue as to the meaning of ambivalence: it is evidently related to the contrast between on the one hand the overvaluing of sexuality in general, and the excremental aspects of sexuality in particular, in the unconscious and in infantile life, and on the other hand the undervaluing of these in consciousness and in adult life. An individual analysis, however, of the infantile origin of all the separate attributes belonging to the salt idea, e.g., the relation of purification to fertilization, though of considerable importance, cannot be undertaken here, for it would lead us too far from the main theme of the work.

Δ

We may now pass to another aspect of the subject, the *etymological* one. It is becoming more and more realized by psychoanalysts that symbolisms gradually formed through "repression" during the progress of civilization leave traces of their original meaning as word deposits. It is even probable that the correctness of the interpretation of a given symbol, such as the one attempted in this essay, could be accurately tested by being submitted to a sufficiently exhaustive comparison with the etymological and semantic history of the words denoting the ideas in question. From this point of view it becomes desirable, therefore, to say a little about the history of the word "salt," though a lack of expert knowledge will necessarily render the present consideration of it very incomplete.

It seems to be definitely established that the names for salt in nearly all European languages find their earliest expression in an old Celtic word which meant "water" or "bog." Schleiden writes as follows:

> The Celts brought with them from their original Indo-Germanic sources some form of the root "sar," which in Sanskrit meant in the first place "to walk," "to go," "to flow," etc., and then in a derived form as "sara" also "river," "water," "sea," "pond." No such word meaning salt is to be found in the Vedas, in the Avesta, nor in any of the cuneiform writings, but in Armenian it occurs as "agh" (*gh* is a common substitute for *l*) thus constituting a bond between "sara" (= water) and the Greek *háls*[188] (= sea-water and salt)...Many words that are either truly Celtic or else have passed through the Celtic language still recall the original meaning of this root word as "sea," "lake," "pond," "pool," "puddle." In Old Irish, *sál* means moor or swamp; *salach* is Old Irish; *halou,* Old Welsh for dirty;[189] the Old High German, Middle High German, and Anglo-Saxon *sol* means a puddle or pool; the sporting words in German, *suhl* (= slough) and *suhlen* (= to wallow), which are used in regard to wild swine; the Low German *solig,* meaning dirty; the French *sale* (= unclean, impure)...The word has always retained a specially close association with the idea of water.[190] In Greek, the word *hals* with an altered gender, feminine, practically means the sea, just as sal did with the Latin poets. Also the rivers which contained salt water or which passed by sources of salt are called by names that in all probability are all related to "salt."[191]

(Schleiden then gives a long list of such rivers and places.)

Hehn suggests that the Greek *sálos* (= *salum*), meaning "bog," "lagoon," "brackish water," belongs to the same series.[192] It originally signified the sea outside the harbor, and thus also the swell of the sea within the harbor; we get here perhaps another hint of the relation between *sal* and *salire* mentioned above.

---

188. The initial *s* has been replaced by *h* only in Greek and Welsh.

189. So the Old Welsh *halog* (= contaminated, impure) and *halou* (= feces).

190. In New Persian also *neme* (= salt) originally meant "moist."

191. Schleiden, *Das Salz,* 15–16.

192. Hehn, *Das Salz,* 125.

It has been suggested[193] that this root word sar was applied to salt to indicate the crackling or spurting of salt when thrown into fire or water, and in support of this it may be added that in the only European languages where the word for salt does not proceed from this root (Lithuanian *druska,* Albanian *kripe*)[194] a word signifying "to strew" is used to denote it. This suggestion is not, however, accepted by any philologist, and it seems certain that the main reason for the use of *sar* was the connotation of the latter as "flowing," "bog," etc., and the resemblance of this to salt-water.

It is thus plain that the original signification of the word was "a dirty fluid." The facts just adduced are certainly striking, and, especially in view of the derivative words that bear the closest relation to the idea of excrement, they may be regarded as an extrinsic confirmation of our conclusion—one which would hardly have been suspected without a detailed investigation—that the idea of salt and water is inherently allied to that of excretion, particularly urine. What was once a conscious association has in the course of centuries become more and more concealed, but though it has disappeared from sight it has in so doing by no means disappeared from existence.

IV.

After this somewhat prolonged excursion we may now return to our original starting-point, namely, the superstitious belief that to spill salt at the table is unlucky. The belief is practically universal and was as prevalent in Ancient Greece and Rome as in Modern Europe.[195] It has been applied to other precious substances besides salt: for instance, in China it is unlucky to spill the contents of an oil jar.[196] In Germany, even to play with salt is unlucky,[197] and for every grain spilt one will have to wait a day (or a week) before heaven's gate.[198]

---

193. Schleiden, *Das Salz,* 17.

194. Hehn, *Das Salz,* 129.

195. Lawrence, *The Magic of the Horse-Shoe,* 167–68.

196. Marian Roalfe Cox, *An Introduction to Folk-Lore* (London: David Nutte, 1904), 10.

197. Wuttke, *Der deutsche Volksaberglaube,* 311.

198. Ibid.

It has been thought that the superstition in question arose from the over-spilling of the salt by Judas at the Last Supper,[199] a rationalistic explanation on a level with that which traces the superstitions concerning the number thirteen to the presence of thirteen at the same meal. Folk beliefs of this order have a far wider and older range than purely Christian ones. The evidence adduced above points unequivocally to a quite different explanation, one which may be indicated by comparing the unlucky act in question with that of Onan described in Genesis (38: 9). In the light of it attention may be directed to the following features of the superstition. Although the spilling of salt is supposed to bring ill luck in general,[200] its specific effect is to destroy friendship[201] and to lead to quarrelling;[202] moreover it brings ill-luck to the person towards whom the salt falls[203] as much as to the one who has spilt it. It acts, in other words, by disturbing the harmony of two people previously engaged in amicable intercourse. From what has been said above about the unconscious symbolism of eating in company it will be intelligible why the spilling of a vital substance at such a moment should be felt to be, somehow or other, a peculiarly unfortunate event. To the unconscious, from which the affective significance arises, it is equivalent on one plane to ejaculatio praecox, and on a more primitive plane to that form of infantile "accident" which psychoanalysis has shown[204] to be genetically related to this unfortunate disorder. The original meaning of the superstition is hinted at in the Prussian belief[205] that to spill salt at a wedding betokens an unhappy marriage, and in the opinion of the "antiques,"[206] who

> thought love decay'd
> When the negligent maid
> Let the salt-cellar tumble before them.

---

199. Lawrence, *The Magic of the Horse-Shoe*, 160, 162.

200. Brand, *Observations on the Popular Antiquities*, 3: 160, 162.

201. Lawrence, *The Magic of the Horse-Shoe*, 169–71.

202. Brand, *loc. cit.*; Lawrence, *The Magic of the Horse-Shoe*, 166–67.

203. Lawrence, *The Magic of the Horse-Shoe*, 166; Brand, *Observations on the Popular Antiquities*, 3: 161–62.

204. Karl Abraham, "Über Ejaculatio praecox," *Internationale Zeitschrift für Psychoanalyse* 4, no. 4 (1916): 171–86.

205. Wuttke, *Der deutsche Volksaberglaube*, 210.

206. Brand, *Observations on the Popular Antiquities*, 3: 163.

It is probable that the ill luck was formerly conceived of as rendering the salt-spiller susceptible to the malevolent influences of evil spirits,[207] and the throwing of salt over the left shoulder, with the idea of averting the ill luck,[208] has been thought to have the object of hitting the invisible demon in the eye and so disabling him.[209] This apparently wild suggestion has its proper meaning, which we need not go into here, but it is more likely that the true object of the proceeding was to make a propitiatory offering to the demon;[210] it has a suspicious resemblance to the Burmese custom of throwing food over the left shoulder in order to conciliate the chief spirit of evil.[211] The maleficium of evil beings is predominantly concerned with interference with sexual relations and disturbances of the sexual functions; I have elsewhere pointed out in detail that the dread of it comes from the fear of impotence.[212] Counter-charms against maleficium largely consist of symbolic acts which either assert the person's potency or serve to re-establish it; instances of both kinds may be found in connection with the averting of evil due to the spilling of salt. In the latter class may be counted the procedure of throwing some of the spilt salt, over the left shoulder, into the fire,[213] the symbol of virility; this custom is still practised in America.[214] To the former class belong the counter-charms of throwing some of the salt out of the window,[215] and of crawling under the table and coming out on the opposite side;[216] to throw something through an aperture, or to crawl through one, symbolizes in folklore, dreams, and mythology the effecting of the sexual act, a symbolism which has given rise to a large group of beliefs and customs.[217]

207. Lawrence, *loc. cit*

208. Dallyel, *The Darker Superstitions of Scotland*, 101.

209. Lawrence, *The Magic of the Horse-Shoe*, 167.

210. Dalyell, *loc. cit.*; Lawrence, *loc. cit.*

211. Lawrence, *loc. cit.*

212. Jones, *Der Alptraum*, 108.

213. Brand, *Observations on the Popular Antiquities*, 3: 161.

214. Clifton Johnson, *What They Say in New England: A Book of Signs, Sayings, and Superstitions* (Boston: Lee and Shepard Publishers, 1896), 92.

215. Wuttke, *Der deutsche Volksaberglaube*, 312.

216. Lawrence, *The Magic of the Horse-Shoe*, 170.

217. Géza Róheim, "The Significance of Stepping Over," *International Journal of Psycho-Analysis* 3, no. 3 (September 1922): 320–26.

The explanation of why the salt has to be thrown *backwards,* and why precisely over the *left* shoulder, would open up themes too extensive for us to enter on here; it is one of the many respects in which the analysis offered in this essay remains incomplete.

V.

Two alternative hypotheses were set forth above concerning the origin of the excessive significance that has so widely been attached to the idea of salt, and it is maintained that the evidence detailed establishes an enormous balance of probability in favor of the second one. According to this, a great part of the significance is derived, not from ideas relating to salt itself but from ideas with which these have been unconsciously associated. Significance has been unconsciously transferred to the subject of salt from emotional sources of the greatest importance to the personality. The natural properties of salt, which in themselves can account for only a part of the feeling with which the salt-idea has been invested, are of such a kind as to render the association of it with another substance of universal import, an easily-made if not an inevitable one. The significance naturally appertaining to such an important and remarkable article of diet as salt has thus been strengthened by an accession of psychical significance derived from deeper sources. Freud's view that superstitions always have a hidden logical meaning, that they constitute a betrayal of unconscious mental processes, is thereby fully confirmed in this particular example, as it has been with all the other superstitions I have investigated. This hidden meaning has the characteristic attributes of the unconscious, notably in its ambivalence, its typically sexual nature, and its close relation to infantile mental processes.

The conclusion reached, therefore, is that *salt is a typical symbol for semen.* But semen itself is ontogenetically not a primary concept, being a replacement of an earlier one concerning urine, and we have correspondingly been able to trace the roots of salt symbolism to an older source than the seminal one. There is every reason to think that the primitive mind equates the idea of salt, not only with that of semen, but also with *the essential constituent of urine.* The idea of salt in folklore and superstition characteristically represents the male, active, fertilizing principle.

The fact that the customs and beliefs relating to salt are exactly parallel to those relating to sexual secretions and excretions, the complex and far-reaching way in which the salt idea is interwoven with matters of sex, particularly with potency and fertilization, the universality of the beliefs in question, the faultless illumination that every detail of the customs and beliefs relating to salt receives as soon as their symbolic signification is recognized, and the impossibility of adequately explaining them on any other basis, are considerations that render it exceedingly difficult to contest the hypothesis here sustained; in fact this can hardly be done except by ignoring the facts adduced above. The validity of the hypothesis rests on the grounds that it completely fulfills both canons of scientific reasoning: it enables one to resume disparate phenomena in a simple formula that renders them more comprehensible, and to predict the occurrence of other, previously unknown phenomena in a way that is susceptible to verification.

The only opposing position that can seriously be maintained is that, however important the association in question may have been in the past, it is no longer operative—except possibly among primitive peoples—so that the only agent responsible for the persistence of the superstition in modern times is the force of meaningless tradition. This raises an extremely important general problem—namely, how far ancient symbolisms are still operative in the minds of civilized people. The tendency of the average layman would be to regard such symbolisms as merely relics from a distant past, and to look upon knowledge concerning them as having no direct bearing on matters of present-day life.

The importance they have, however, is far from being a simply antiquarian one.[218] Psychoanalytic investigation has shown not only that symbolism plays a much more extensive part in mental functioning than was previously imagined, but also that there is a pronounced tendency for the same symbolisms to recur quite independently of the influence

---

218. Roughly speaking, it may be said that owing to the action of "repression" the sexual meaning of such symbolisms retreats from view during the development of civilization in much the same way as it does during the development of the individual. In both cases, however, the retreating from view means only a disappearance from consciousness, not from existence.

of other people. This is in entire accord with modern mythological and anthropological research,[219] since it is known that identical symbolisms occur in different parts of the world, and in different ages, in circumstances that preclude the possibility of their having been merely transmitted from one place to another. There appears to be a general tendency of the human mind to symbolize objects and interests of paramount. and universal significance in forms that are psychologically the most suitable and available. That these stereotyped forms of symbolism are produced quite spontaneously is a matter capable of direct demonstration. One finds, for instance, a country farmer unconsciously exhibiting in his dreams, in his mental reactions, and in his psycho-neurotic symptoms the identical symbolisms that played a part in the religions of Ancient India or Greece, and in a way so foreign to the conscious life of his environment as to exclude with certainty any course in either suggestion or tradition. In my observations of the seminal symbolism of salt, for instance, with actual patients I have come across reactions indicating unconscious attitudes of mind exactly comparable to that implied in many of the antiquated practices detailed earlier in this essay.

The most that these external influences can accomplish is to direct the unconscious process into a given form, but it cannot maintain this direction of interest unless the form of symbolism assumed becomes linked with a spontaneous interest of the individual. Thus, a person brought up in a society that took no interest in a given superstition would be less likely to develop the superstition himself than if brought up in a different society—though he might easily do so, nevertheless, especially if he were of the obsessional type of mind; but—and this is the important point—a person brought up in however superstitious a society would not develop a given superstition unless it was of such a kind as to be capable

---

219. It will be gathered from the whole tone of the present essay that the author attaches especial importance to the interrelation of psychoanalytic and anthropological research. The anthropologist's material is rendered much more intelligible by psychoanalysis, and his views can there be submitted to verifiable tests with actual individual minds, while on the other hand through this material the psycho-analytical conclusions receive extensive confirmation, correction, and amplification. The comparative study of both fields is mutually instructive, and much is to be expected in the future from the work of men such as Róheim who are equally trained in both fields.

of being associated to his personal mental complexes. This association is a purely individual one, and without it the superstitious belief fails to appeal; it need hardly be said that the process, particularly in civilized communities, is most often entirely unconscious. To put the matter more concretely: what is meant is that with every person who has made his own a superstitious practice regarding salt, who follows it from an inner motive, from a "superstitious feeling"—even though he might consciously maintain that he did not believe in it—analysis would show that the idea of salt was symbolizing the idea of semen (or urine) in his unconscious mind, that this association was a personal one of his own.

The reason why certain superstitions are so widely prevalent is because the ideas are such as to render easily possible the forging of associations between them and personal ideas of general interest and significance. The conditions, however, have their definite limitations: the forging of the associations must not be either too easy or too difficult. From this point of view one may venture to suggest that the general decline of superstition among educated classes is not entirely due—as is commonly thought-to the more enlightened intelligence of such classes, but is also in part due to their greater cultural inhibition of symbolical thinking in general, and of sexual symbolism in particular.

A superstition such as that of salt-spilling is usually dismissed either as being too trivial to warrant the dignity of an explanation, or else with one that is obviously superficial and inadequate. Even in the opinions on the subject enunciated in psychological textbooks the writer often gives the impression of having dispensed with an investigation sufficiently detailed to establish their validity. On the other hand, attentive consideration of any given superstition reveals how much we have to learn about the subject, and demonstrates that it is often, as in the present instance, connected with aspects of the human mind that are of fundamental importance. A psychology of religion, for example, is impossible without an understanding of superstition. Here, as elsewhere, Freud has shown that a byway in psychology may lead to country that yields an unexpectedly rich harvest.

Sal

A. *Salt as the Arcane Substance*

In this section I shall discuss not only salt but a number of symbolisms that are closely connected with it. [...] This explains the length of the present entire chapter: extensive digressions are necessary in order to do justice to the various aspects of the unconscious that are expressed by salt, and at the same time to explain their psychological meaning.

Owing to the theory of "correspondentia," regarded as axiomatic in the Middle Ages, the principles of each of the four worlds—the intelligible or divine, the heavenly, the earthly, and the infernal[1]—corresponded to each other. Usually, however, there was a division into three worlds to correspond with the Trinity: heaven, earth, hell.[2] Triads were also known in alchemy. From the time of Paracelsus the most important triad was Sulphur-Mercurius-Sal, which was held to correspond with the Trinity. Georg von Welling, the plagiarist of Johann Rudolf Glauber, still thought in 1735 that his triad of fire, sun, and salt[3] was "in its root entirely one thing."[4] The use of the Trinity formula in alchemy is so common that further documentation is unnecessary. A subtle feature of the Sulphur-Mercurius-Sal formula is that the central figure, Mercurius, is by nature

---

1. Blasius Vigenerus [Blaise de Vigenère], in *Tractatus de igne & sale* (*Theatrum chemicum*, 6 vols. [Oberursel and Strasbourg: Lazarus Zetzner and heirs, 1602–61], 6: 32 f.), speaks of three worlds. The fire on earth corresponds to the sun in heaven, and this to the Spiritus Sanctus "in the intelligible world." But on p. 39 he suddenly remembers the fourth, forgotten world: "The fourth is infernal, opposed to the intelligible, glowing and burning without any light." He also distinguishes four kinds of fire. (Cf. *CW* 9.2: *Aion: Researches into the Phenomenology of the Self,* pars. 203, 393, and n. 81.)

2. Heaven-earth-hell (like sulphur-mercurius-sal) is a false triad: earth is dual, consisting of the light-world above and the shadow-world below.

3. Fire = sulphur, Sol = Mercurius (as the mother and son of Sol).

4. Georg von Welling, *Opus Mago-Cabbalisticum et Theosophicum* (Homburg vor der Höhe: Joh. Phillip Helwig, 1735), 30.

androgynous and thus partakes both of the masculine red sulphur and of the lunar salt.[5] His equivalent in the celestial realm is the planetary pair Sol and Luna, and in the "intelligible" realm Christ in his mystical androgyny, the "man encompassed by the woman,"[6] i.e., *sponsus* and *sponsa* (Ecclesia). Like the Trinity, the alchemical "triunity" is a quaternity in disguise owing to the duplicity of the central figure: Mercurius is not only split into a masculine and a feminine half, but is the poisonous dragon and at the same time the heavenly lapis. This makes it clear that the dragon is analogous to the devil and the lapis to Christ, in accordance with the ecclesiastical view of the devil as an autonomous counterpart of Christ. Furthermore, not only the dragon but the negative aspect of sulphur, namely *sulphur comburens,* is identical with the devil, as Glauber says:[7] "Verily, sulphur is the true black devil of hell, who can be conquered by no element save by salt alone." Salt by contrast is a "light" substance, similar to the lapis, as we shall see.

---

5. A quotation from Hermes in *Rosarium philosophorum, in Artis auriferae quam chemiam vocant,* 2 vols. [Basel: Conrad Waldkirch, 1593], 2: 244, mentions "Sale nostrae lunariae" (the salt of our moon-plant). "Our salt is found in a certain precious Salt, and in all things. On this account the ancient Philosophers called it the common moon," *Musaeum hermeticum* (Frankfurt: Hermann à Sande, 1678), 217; *HM* 1: 77. The salt from the Polar Sea is "lunar" (feminine), and the salt from the Equatorial Sea is "solar" (masculine): Von Welling, *Opus Mago-Cabbalisticum,* 17. Johann Rudolph Glauber (*Tractatus de signatura salium, metallorum, et planetarum* [Amsterdam: Johann Janssonius, 1659], 11) calls salt feminine and gives Eve as a parallel.

6. "Femina circumdabit virum" (Jeremiah 31: 22). Gregory I, *In primun Regum expositiones,* Lib. 1 (*PL* 79: 23). This idea is developed in literal form, in both Tibetan and Bengali Tantrism, as Shiva in the embrace of Shakti, the maker of Maya. We find the same idea in alchemy. Johann Daniel Mylius (*Philosophia reformata* [Frankfurt, 1622], 8–9) says: "[God has] love all round him. Others have declared him to be an intellectual and fiery spirit, having no form, but transforming himself into whatsoever he wills and making himself equal to all things ... Whence, by a kind of similitude to the nature of the soul, we give to God, or the power of God that sustains all things, the name of *Anima media natura* or soul of the World (*Animam medium naturam, aut animam Mundi appellamus*)." The concluding words are a quotation from *De arte chimica* (*Art. aurif.,* 1: 608).

7. Johann Rudolph Glauber, *Tractatus de natura salium* (Amsterdam: Johann Janssonius, 1659), 26ff.

From all this we get the following schema:

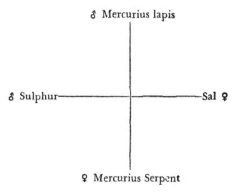

Here we have another of those well-known quaternities of Opposites which are usually masked as a triad, just as the Christian Trinity is able to maintain itself as such only by eliminating the fourth protagonist of the divine drama. If he were included there would be, not a Trinity, but a Christian Quaternity. For a long time there had been a psychological need for this, as is evident from the medieval pictures of the Assumption and Coronation of the Virgin; it was also responsible for elevating her to the position of mediatrix, corresponding to Christ's position as the mediator, with the difference that Mary only transmits grace but does not generate it. The recent promulgation of the dogma of the Assumption emphasizes the taking up not only of the soul but of the body of Mary into the Trinity, thus making a dogmatic reality of those medieval representations of the quaternity which are constructed on the following pattern:

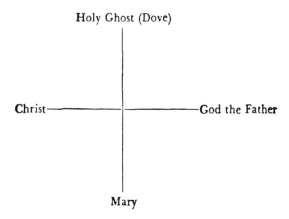

Only in 1950, after the teaching authority in the Church had long deferred it, and almost a century after the declaration of the dogma of the Immaculate Conception, did the Pope, moved by a growing wave of popular petitions,[8] feel compelled to declare the Assumption as a revealed truth. All the evidence shows that the dogmatization was motivated chiefly by the religious need of the Catholic masses. Behind this stands the archetypal numen of feminine deity,[9] who, at the Council of Ephesus in 431, imperiously announced her claim to the title of "Theotokos" (God-bearer), as distinct from that of a mere "Anthropotokos" (man-bearer) accorded to her by the Nestorian rationalists.

The taking up of the body had long been emphasized as an historical and material event, and the alchemists could therefore make use of the representations of the Assumption in describing the glorification of matter in the Opus. The illustration of this process in Reusner's *Pandora*[10] shows, underneath the coronation scene, a kind of shield between the emblems of Matthew and Luke, on which is depicted the extraction of Mercurius from the *prima materia*. The extracted spirit appears in monstrous form: the head is surrounded by a halo, and reminds us of the traditional head of Christ, but the arms are snakes and the lower half of the body resembles a stylized fish's tail.[11] This is without doubt the *anima*

---

8. "During the course of time such postulations and petitions did not decrease but rather grew continually in number and in urgency." Pius XII, *Munificentissimus Deus* [online at *https://www.vatican.va/content/pius-xii/en/apost_constitutions/documents/hf_p-xii_apc_19501101_munificentissimus-deus.html*].

9. A Catholic writer says of the Assumption: "Nor, would it seem, is the underlying motif itself even peculiarly Christian; rather would it seem to be but one expression of a universal archetypal pattern, which somehow responds to some deep and widespread human need, and which finds other similar expressions in countless myths and rituals, poems and pictures, practices and even philosophies, all over the globe." Victor White, "The Scandal of the Assumption," *Life of the Spirit* 5, no. 53/54 (November-December 1950): 200.

10. (Hieronymus Reusner, *Pandora: Das ist die edleste Gab Gottes / oder der Werde und heilsame Stein der Weysen* (Basel: Sebastian Henric Petri, 1588), 253; *CW* 12: *Psychology and Alchemy*, fig. 232.

11. Cf. the man with a fish's tail in the mosaic on the floor of the cathedral of Pesaro, 6th cent., with the inscription *Est homo non totus medius, sed piscis ab imo* (This man is not complete, but half fish below). Ferdinand Becker, *Die Darstellung Jesu Christi*

mundi who has been freed from the shackles of matter, the *filius macro-cosmi* or Mercurius-Anthropos, who, because of his double nature, is not only spiritual and physical but unites in himself the morally highest and lowest.[12] The illustration in the *Pandora* points to the great secret which the alchemists dimly felt was implicit in the Assumption. The proverbial darkness of sublunary matter has always been associated with the "prince of this world," the devil. He is the metaphysical figure who is excluded from the Trinity, but who, as the counterpart of Christ, is the *sine qua non* of the drama of redemption.[13] His equivalent in alchemy is the dark side of Mercurius duplex and, as we saw, the active sulphur. He also conceals himself in the poisonous dragon, the preliminary, chthonic form of the *lapis aethereus*. To the natural philosophers of the Middle Ages, and to Dorn in particular, it was perfectly clear that the triad must be comple-mented by a fourth, as the lapis had always been regarded as a quaternity of elements. It did not disturb them that this would necessarily involve the evil spirit. On the contrary, the dismemberment and self-devour-ing of the dragon probably seemed to them a commendable operation. Dorn, however, saw in the quaternity the absolute opposite of the Trin-ity, namely the female principle, which seemed to him "of the devil," for which reason he called the devil the "four-horned serpent." This insight must have given him a glimpse into the core of the problem.[14] In his ref-utation he identified woman with the devil because of the number two, which is characteristic of both. The devil, he thought, was the binarius itself, since it was created on the second day of Creation, on Monday, the day of the moon, on which God failed to express his pleasure, this being the day of "doubt" and separation.[15] Dorn puts into words what is merely hinted at in the *Pandora* illustration.

unter dem Bilde des Fisches auf den Monumenten der Kirche der Katakomben (Breslau: Max Mälzer, 1866), 127.

12. Cf. "The Spirit Mercurius," *CW* 13: *Alchemical Studies,* pars. 267 ff.; also the arcane teaching of Paracelsus in "Paracelsus as a Spiritual Phenomenon," ibid., pars. 159ff.

13. Cf. "A Psychological Approach to the Dogma of the Trinity," *CW* 11: *Psychology and Religion: West and East,* pars. 248f., 252ff.

14. For a closer discussion, see "Psychology and Religion," ibid., pars. 104ff.

15. *De tenebris contra naturam* (*Theatr. chem.,* 1: 527). Cf. "Psychology and Religion," pars. 104, n.47, 120, n. 11, and "A Psychological Approach to the Dogma of the Trinity," par. 262.

If we compare this train of thought with the Christian quaternity which
the new dogma has virtually produced (but has not defined as such), it will
immediately be apparent that we have here an "upper" quaternio, which is
supraordinate to man's wholeness and psychologically comparable to the
Moses quaternio of the Gnostics.[16] Man and the dark abyss of the world,
the *deus absconditus,* have not yet been taken up into it. Alchemy, however,
is the herald of a still-unconscious drive for maximal integration which
seems to be reserved for a distant future, even though it originated with
Origen's doubt concerning the ultimate fate of the devil.[17]

In philosophical alchemy, salt is a cosmic principle. According to its
position in the quaternity, it is correlated with the feminine, lunar side and
with the upper, light half. It is therefore not surprising that Sal is one of
the many designations for the arcane substance. This connotation seems
to have developed in the early Middle Ages under Arabic influence. The
oldest traces of it can be found in the *Turba,* where salt-water and sea-
water are synonyms for the *aqua permanens,*[18] and in Senior, who says that
Mercurius is made from salt.[19] His treatise is one of the earliest authori-
ties in Latin alchemy. Here, "Sal Alkali" also plays the role of the arcane
substance, and Senior mentions that the *dealbatio* was called "salsatura"
(marination).[20] In the almost equally old *Allegoriae sapientum,* the *lapis* is
described as "salsus" (salty).[21] Arnaldus de Villanova (1235?–1313) says:
"Whoever possesses the salt that can be melted, and the oil that cannot be
burned, may praise God."[22] It is clear from this that salt is an arcane substance. The *Rosarium,* which leans very heavily on the old Latin sources,
remarks that the "whole secret lies in the prepared common salt,"[23] and

---

16. For details, see *CW* 9.2: *Aion,* pars. 359ff.

17. Ibid., par. 171, n.29.

18. Julius Ruska, *Turba Philosophorum: Ein Beitrag zur Geschichte der Alchemie* (Berlin
and Heidelberg: Springer-Verlag, 1931), 283.

19. "Primo fit cinis, postea sal, & de illo sale per diversas operationes Mercurius
Philosophorum" (First comes the ash, then the salt, and from that salt by divers operations the Mercury of the Philosophers." Quoted in *Clangor buccinae* (*Art. aurif.,* 1: 488).

20. *De chemia* (*Theatr. chem.,* 5: 231). For "salsatura," see *Aurora consurgens II* (*Art.
aurif.,* 1: 205).

21. *Theatr. chem.,* 5: 77.

22. Cited in *Rosarium phil.* (*Art. aurif.,* 2: 244).

23. Ibid.

that the "root of the art is the soap of the sages" (*sapo sapientum*), which is the "mineral" of all salts and is called the "bitter salt" (*sal amarum*).[24] Whoever knows the salt knows the secret of the old sages.[25] "Salts and alums are the helpers of the Stone."[26] Isaac Hollandus calls salt the medium between the *terra sulphurea* and the water. "God poured a certain salt into them in order to unite them, and the sages named this salt the salt of the wise."[27]

Among later writers, salt is even more clearly the arcane substance. For Mylius it is synonymous with the tincture;[28] it is the earth-dragon who eats his own tail, and the "ash," the "diadem of thy heart."[29] The "salt of the metals" is the lapis.[30] Basilius Valentin us speaks of a "sal spirituale."[31] It is the seat of the virtue which makes the "art" possible,[32] the "most noble treasury,"[33] the "good and noble salt," which "though it has not the form of salt from the beginning, is nevertheless called salt;" it "becomes impure and pure of itself, it dissolves and coagulates itself, or, as the sages say, locks and unlocks itself;"[34] it is the "quintessence, above all things and in all creatures."[35] "The whole magistery lies in the

---

24. Ibid., 222. The same on p. 225, where the salt is also called the "key that closes and opens [*claviculam quae claudit & aperit*]."

25. *Rosarium phil.* (*Art. aurif.*, 2: 244).

26. Ibid., 269. The text adds: "He who tastes not the savor of the salts, shall never come to the desired ferment of the ferment [*ad optatum fermentum fermenti*]."

27. *Opera mineralia* (*Theatr. chem.*, 3: 411).

28. Mylius, *Phil. ref.*, 189.

29. Ibid., 195.

30. Ibid., 222. Also in *Rosarium phil.* (*Art. aurif.*, 2: 208; Heinrich Khunrath, *Amphitheatrum sapientiae aeternae* (Hanau: Wilhelm Anton, 1609), 194. and *Mus. herm.*, 20; *HM* 1: 22.

31. Cited in *Tractatus aureus* (*Mus. herm.*, 31; *HM* 1: 32). The writings of Basilius Valentinus do not date from the 15th century, but are a 17th-century forgery.

32. "Alexander the Great, King of Macedonia, in his Philosophy has the following words: "Blessed be God in heaven who has created this art in the Salt [*Benedictus Deus incoelo siet qui artem hanc in Sale creavit*]," *Gloria mundi* (*Mus. herm.*, 217; *HM* 1: 176–77).

33. *Mus. herm.*, 218; *HM* 1: 177.

34. *Mus. herm.*, 216; *HM* 1: 176.

35. *Mus. herm.*, 217; *HM* 1: 177. It is also described as the "balsam of nature" (Heinrich Khunrath, *Vom Hylealischen, das ist pri-materialischen catholischen oder algemeinen*

salt and its solution."[36] The "permanent radical moisture" consists of salt.[37] It is synonymous with the "incombustible oil,"[38] and is altogether a mystery to be concealed.[39]

As the arcane substance, it is identified with various synonyms for the latter. Above all it is an "ens centrale." For Khunrath, salt is the "physical center of the earth."[40] For Vigenerus, it is a component of "that virginal and pure earth which is contained in the center of all composite elementals, or in the depths of the same."[41] Glauber calls salt the "concentrated center of the elements."[42]

Although the arcane substance is usually identified with Mercurius, the relation of salt to Mercurius is seldom mentioned. Senior, as we noted, says that "by divers operations" Mercurius is made from salt,[43] and Khunrath identifies Mercurius with common salt.[44] The rarity of the identification strikes us just because the "salt of the wise" really implies its relation to Mercurius. I can explain this only on the supposition that salt did not acquire its significance until later times and then at once appeared as an independent figure in the Sulphur-Mercurius-Sal triad.

Salt also has an obvious relation to the earth, not to the earth as such, but to "our earth," by which is naturally meant the arcane substance.[45] This is evident from the aforementioned identification of salt with the earth-dragon. The full text of Mylius runs:

---

natürlichen Chaos der naturgemessen Alchymiae und Alchymisten [Magdeburg: Johann Francken, 1616], 258) and as the "fifth element" (*mare*, sea) (*De igne & sale* [*Theatr. chem.*, 6: 122]).

36. Khunrath, *Vom Hylealischen*, 256.

37. Ibid., 257.

38. Ibid., 260.

39. Khunrath, *Amphitheatrum*, 194.

40. Khunrath, *Vom Hylealischen*, 257.

41. *De igne & sale* (*Theatr. chem.*, 6: 44).

42. Glauber, *Tract. de natura salium*, 44. Glauber adds the verse: "In the salt and fire / Lies the treasure so dear."

43. *Art. aurif.*, 1: 210. In the *Turba*, salt-water and sea-water are synonyms for Mercurius.

44. Khunrath, *Vom Hylealischen*, 257.

45. "Our salt, that is to say, our earth," *Tract. aureus* (*Mus. herm.*, 20; *HM* 1: 22). Cf. also *Clangor buccinae* (*Art. aurif.*, 1: 488) and *Scala philosophorum* (*Art. aurif.*, 2: 107).

What remains below in the retort is our salt, that is, our earth, and it
is of a black color, a dragon that eats his own tail. For the dragon is
the matter that remains behind after the distillation of water from it,
and this water is called the dragon's tail, and the dragon is its blackness, and the dragon is saturated with his water and coagulated, and
so he eats his tail.[46]

The rarely mentioned relation of salt to the *nigredo*[47] is worth noting here,
for because of its proverbial whiteness salt is constantly associated with
the *albedo*. On the other hand, we would expect the close connection
between salt and water, which is in fact already implicit in the sea-water.
The *aqua pontica* plays an important role as a synonym for the *aqua permanens*, as also does "mare" (sea). That salt, as well as Luna, is an essential
component of this is clear from Vigenerus: "There is nothing wherein
the moisture lasts longer, or is wetter, than salt, of which the sea for the
most part consists. Neither is there anything wherein the moon displays
her motion more clearly than the sea, as can be seen from its ebb and
flow." Salt, he says, has an "inexterminable humidity," and "that is the reason why the sea cannot be dried up."[48] Khunrath identifies the *femina
alba* or *candida* with the "crystalline salt," and this with the white water.[49]
"Our water" cannot be made without salt,[50] and without salt the opus will
not succeed.[51] According to Rupescissa (ca. 1350), salt is "water which
the dryness of the fire has coagulated."[52]

B. *The Bitterness*

Inseparable from salt and sea is the quality of *amaritudo,* "bitterness." The
etymology of Isidore of Seville was accepted all through the Middle Ages:
"Mare ab amaro."[53] Among the alchemists the bitterness became a kind of

46. Mylius, *Phil. ref.,* 195.

47. One place is in *Gloria mundi* (*Mus. herm.,* 216; *HM* 1: 176): "(In the beginning) it
is mostly black and evil smelling [*(In initio) Sal est nigrum ac foetidum*]."

48. *De igne & sale* (*Theatr. chem.,* 6: 98).

49. Khunrath, *Vom Hylealischen,* 197f.

50. Ibid., 229.

51. Ibid., 254.

52. *De confectione lapidis* (*Theatr. chem.,* 3: 199).

53. Isidore of Seville [Isidorus Hispalensis], *Liber etymologiarum,* 13: 14, fol. lxviiiv.

technical term. Thus, in the treatise *Rosinus ad Euthiciam*,[54] there is the following dialogue between Zosimos and Theosebeia: "This is the stone that hath in it glory and color. And she: Whence cometh its color? He replied: From its exceeding strong bitterness. And she: Whence cometh its bitterness and intensity? He answered: From the impurity of its metal." The treatise *Rosini ad Sarratantam episcopum* says: "Take the stone that is black, white, red, and yellow, and is a wonderful bird that flies without wings in the blackness of the night and the brightness of the day: in the bitterness that is in its throat the coloring will be found."[55] "Each thing in its first matter is corrupt and bitter," says Ripley. "The bitterness is a tincturing poison."[56] And Mylius: "Our stone is endowed with the strongest spirit, bitter and brazen (*aeneus*);"[57] and the *Rosarium* mentions that salt is bitter because it comes from the "mineral of the sea."[58] The "Liber Alze"[59] says: "O nature of this wondrous thing, which transforms the body into spirit!...When it is found alone it conquers all things, and is an excellent, harsh, and bitter acid, which transmutes gold into pure spirit."[60]

These quotations clearly allude to the sharp taste of salt and seawater. The reason why the taste is described as bitter and not simply as salt may lie first of all in the inexactness of the language, since *amarus* also means "sharp," "biting," "harsh," and is used metaphorically for acrimonious speech or a wounding joke. Besides this, the language of the Vulgate had an important influence as it was one of the main sources for medieval Latin. The moral use which the Vulgate consistently makes of *amarus* and *amaritudo* gives them, in alchemy as well, a nuance that cannot be passed over. This comes out clearly in Ripley's remark that "each thing in its first matter is corrupt and bitter." The juxtaposition of

54. A corrupt version of *Zosimos ad Theosebeiam*, owing to Arabic-Latin transmission (*Art. aurif.*, 1 : 264).

55. *Art. aurif.*, 1 : 316. Cf. also *Ros. phil.* (*Art. aurif.*, 2 : 258); Mylius, *Phil. ref.*, 249; *Tract. aureus* (*Ars chemica quod sit licita recte exercentibus, probationes doctissimorum iurisconsultorum* [Strasbourg: Samuel Emmel 1566], 11 f.).

56. George Ripley, *Chymische Schrifften* (Erfurt: Johan Birkner, 1624), 100.

57. Mylius, *Phil. ref.*, 244. The same in *Ros. phil.* (*Art. aurif.*, 2: 248).

58. *Ros. phil.* (*Art. aurif.*, 2: 222).

59. *Mus. herm.*, 328; *HM* 1 : 263f.).

60. A *Turba* quotation from Sermo XV of Flritis (or Fictes=Socrates). See Ruska, *Turba philosophorum*, 124f.

these two attributes indicates the inner connection between them: corruption and bitterness are on the same footing, they denote the state of imperfect bodies, the initial state of the *prima materia*. Among the best known synonyms for the latter are the "chaos" and the "sea," in the classical, mythological sense denoting the beginning of the world, the sea in particular being conceived as the παμμήτηρ, "matrix of all creatures."[61] The *prima materia* is often called *aqua pontica*. The salt that "comes from the mineral of the sea" is by its very nature bitter, but the bitterness is due also to the impurity of the imperfect body. This apparent contradiction is explained by the report of Plutarch that the Egyptians regarded the sea as something impure and untrustworthy (μηδέ σύμφυλον αὐτῆς) and as the domain of Typhon (Set); they called salt the "spume of Typhon."[62] In his *Philosophia reformata*, Mylius mentions "sea spume" together with the "purged or purified" sea, rock salt, the bird, and Luna as equivalent synonyms for the *lapis occultus*.[63] Here the impurity of the sea is indirectly indicated by the epithets "purged" or "purified." The sea-spume is on a par with the salt and—of particular interest—with the bird, naturally the bird of Hermes, and this throws a sudden light on the above passage from Rosinus, about the bird with bitterness in its throat. The bird is a parallel of salt because salt is a spirit,[64] a volatile substance, which the alchemists were wont to conceive as a bird.

As the expulsion of the spirit was effected by various kinds of burning (*combustio, adustio, calcinatio, assatio, sublimatio, incineratio*, etc.), it was

---

61. Cf. *CW* 12: *Psychology and Alchemy*, pars. 56f., 476.

62. "Isis and Osiris," in *Moralia* 5, Loeb Classical Library 306, translated by Frank Cole Babbit (Cambridge, Mass.: Harvard University Press, 1936), 79.

63. Mylius, *Phil. ref.*, 305. The text is a poem that Mylius cites from an older source. The most important passages are the following:

There is a secret stone, hidden in a deep well
Worthless and rejected, concealed in dung or filth...
And this stone is a bird, and neither stone nor bird...
...now sea-spume or vinegar
Now again the gem of salt [*gemma salis*], Almisadir the common salt [*sal generalis*]...
Now the sea, cleansed and purged with sulphur.

At that time, *gemma* simply meant "stone." Cf. Martin Ruland, *Lexicon alchemiae sive dictionarum alchemisticum* (Frankfurt: Zacharias Palthenius, 1622), 241f.

64. Cf. above: "Our stone is endowed with the strongest spirit."

natural to call the end product "ash"—again in a double sense as *scoria, faex,* etc., and as the spirit or bird of Hermes. Thus the *Rosarium* says: "Sublime with fire, until the spirit which thou wilt find in it [the substance] goeth forth from it, and it is named the bird or the ash of Hermes. Therefore saith Morienus: "Despise not the ashes, for they are the diadem of thy heart, and the ash of things that endure."[65] In other words, the ash is the spirit that dwells in the glorified body.

This bird or spirit is associated with various colors. At first the bird is black, then it grows white feathers, which finally become colored.[66] The Chinese cousin of the *avis Hermetis,* the "scarlet bird," moults in a similar way.[67] We are told in the treatise of Wei Po-yang: "The fluttering Chuniao flies the five colors."[68] They are arranged as follows:

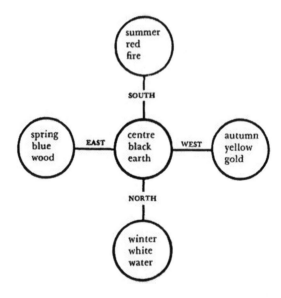

65. *Art. aurif.,* 2: 282f.

66. Cf. Christian Rosencreutz, *The Hermetick Romance or The Chymical Wedding,* translated by E. Foxcroft (London: A. Sowle 1690), 155.

67. The phoenix, the Western equivalent of this wonder-bird, is described by Maier as very colorful: "His neck is surrounded with a golden brightness [*aureus fulgor*], and the rest of his body by feathers of purple hue [*purpureus color*]," Michael Maier, *Symbola aureae mensae* (Frankfurt: Lucas Jennis, 1617), 598.

68. Lu-Chiang Wu, Tenney L. Davis, and Wei Po-yang, "An Ancient Chinese Treatise on Alchemy Entitled Ts'an T'ung Ch'i," *Isis* 18, no. 2 (October 1932): 218, 258.

Earth occupies the central position as the fifth element, though it is not the quintessence and goal of the work but rather its basis, corresponding to terra as the arcane substance in Western alchemy.[69]

As regards the origin and meaning of the *avis Hermetis,* I would like to mention the report of Aelian that the ibis is "dear to Hermes, the father of words, since in its form it resembles the nature of the Logos; for its blackness and swift flight could be compared to the silent and introverted (ἔνθον ἐπιστρεφομένῳ) Logos, but its whiteness to the Logos already uttered and heard, which is the servant and messenger of the inner word."[70]

It is not easy for a modern mind to conceive salt, a cold-damp, lunar-terrestrial substance, as a bird and a spirit. Spirit, as the Chinese conceive it, is yang, the fiery and dry element, and this accords with the views of Heraclitus as well as with the Christian concept of the Holy Ghost as tongues of fire. Luna, we have seen, is unquestionably connected with *mens, manas,* mind, etc. But these connections are of a somewhat ambiguous nature. Although the earth can boast of an earth-spirit and other daemons, they are after all "spirits" and not "spirit." The "cold" side of nature is not lacking in spirit, but it is a spirit of a special kind, which Christianity regarded as demonic and which therefore found no acclaim except in the realm of the magical arts and sciences. This spirit is the snake-like Nous or Agathodaimon, which in Hellenistic syncretism merges together with Hermes. Christian allegory and iconography also took possession of it on the basis of John 3: 14: "And as Moses lifted up the serpent in the wilderness, even so must the Son of man be lifted up." The mercurial serpent or "Spirit Mercurius" is the personification and living continuation of the spirit who, in the prayer entitled the "Secret Inscription" in the Great Magic Papyrus of Paris, is invoked as follows:

> Greetings, entire edifice of the Spirit of the air, greetings, Spirit that penetratest from heaven to earth, and from earth, which abideth in the

---

69. It is strange that the editors of Wei Po-yang are of the opinion that no fundamental analogy obtains between Chinese and Western Alchemy. The similarity is, on the contrary, amazing. [Cf. "Concerning Mandala Symbolism," *CW* 9.1: *The Archetypes and the Collective Unconscious,* pars. 630ff. (figs. 1–3).]

70. *De natura animalium,* Lib. XVII, edited by Rudolph Hercher (Leipzig: B. G. Teubner, 1864), 1.257.

midst of the universe, to the uttermost bounds of the abyss, greetings, Spirit that penetratest into me, and shakest me...Greetings, beginning and end of irremovable nature, greetings, thou who revolvest the elements that untiringly render service, greetings to thee from the sun thy servant, glorifier of the world, greetings to thee from the moon shining by night with disc of fickle brilliance, greetings to thee from all spirits of the demons of the air...O great, greatest, spherical, incomprehensible fabric of the world,...thou that hast the form of aether, of water, of earth, of wind, of light, of darkness, glittering like a star, damp-fiery-cold Spirit [ὑγροπυρινοψυχρὸν πνεῦμα]![71]

Here is a magnificent description of a spirit that is apparently the exact opposite of the Christian pneuma. This antique spirit is also the spirit of alchemy, which today we can interpret as the unconscious projected into heavenly space and external objects. Although declared to be the devil by the early Christians, it should not be identified outright with evil; it merely has the uncomfortable quality of being beyond good and evil, and it gives this perilous quality to anyone who identifies with it, as we can see from the eloquent case of Nietzsche and the psychic epidemic that came after him. This spirit that is "beyond good and evil" is not the same as being "six thousand feet above good and evil," but rather the same distance below it, or better, before it. It is the spirit of the chaotic waters of the beginning, before the second day of Creation, before the separation of the opposites and hence before the advent of consciousness. That is why it leads those whom it overcomes neither upwards nor beyond, but back into chaos. This spirit corresponds to that part of the psyche which has not been assimilated to consciousness and whose transformation and integration are the outcome of a long and wearisome opus. The artifex was, in his way, conscious enough of the dangers of the work, and for this reason his operations consisted largely of precautions whose equivalents are the rites of the Church.

The alchemists understood the return to chaos as an essential part of the opus. It was the stage of the *nigredo* and *mortificatio,* which was then followed by the "purgatorial fire" and the *albedo.* The spirit of chaos is

---

71. *Papyri Graecae Magicae: Die griechischen Zauberpapyri,* edited and translated by Karl Preisendanz, 2 vols. (Leipzig and Berlin: B. G. Teubner, 1928–31), 1: 110 (Pap. IV.1115–66).

indispensable to the work, and it cannot be distinguished from the "gift of the Holy Ghost" any more than the Satan of the Old Testament can be distinguished from Yahweh. The unconscious is both good and evil and yet neither, the matrix of all potentialities.

After these remarks—which seemed to me necessary—on the "salt-spirit," as Khunrath calls it, let us turn back to the *amaritudo.* As the bitter salt comes from the impure sea, it is understandable that the *Gloria mundi* should call it "mostly black and evil-smelling in the beginning.[72] The blackness and bad smell, described by the alchemists as the "stench of the graves," pertain to the underworld and to the sphere of moral darkness. This impure quality is common also to the *corruptio,* which, as we saw, Ripley equates with bitterness. Vigenerus describes salt as "corruptible," in the sense that the body is subject to corruption and decay and does not have the fiery and incorruptible nature of the spirit.[73]

The moral use of qualities that were originally physical is clearly dependent, particularly in the case of a cleric like Ripley, on ecclesiastical language. About this I can be brief, as I can rely on [Hugo] Rahner's valuable "Antenna Crucis: II. Das Meer der Welt" [*Zeitschrift für katholische Theologie* 66, no. 2/3 (1942): 89–118]. Here Rahner brings together all the patristic allegories that are needed to understand the alchemical symbolism. The patristic use of "mare" is defined by St. Augustine: "Mare saeculum est" (the sea is the world).[74] It is the "essence of the world, as the element...subject to the devil." St. Hilary says: "By the depths of the sea is meant the seat of hell."[75] The sea is the "gloomy abyss," the remains of the original pit,[76] and hence of the chaos that covered the earth. For St. Augustine this abyss is the realm of power allotted to the devil and demons

---

72. *Mus. herm.,* 216; *HM* 1: 176.

73. "To the spiritual [body] is referred fire, to the corruptible [body], Salt [*Ad hoc, scl. (corpus) spirituale, ignis, ad illus vero scl. corruptibile Sal*]," *De igne & sale* (*Theatr. chem.,* 6: 7).

74. St. Augustine, *Expositions of the Book of Psalms* (Oxford: John Henry Parker, 1847–57), 4: 340 (Ps. 92: 7).

75. "Profundum maris sedem intelligamus inferni," Hilary of Poutiers, *Tractatus super Psalmos* 28 (*PL* 9: col. 487).

76. Rahner, "Antennae Crucis," 105.

after their fall.[77] It is on the one hand a "deep that cannot be reached or comprehended"[78] and on the other the "depths of sin."[79] For Gregory the Great the sea is the "depths of eternal death."[80] Since ancient times it was the "abode of waterdemons."[81] There dwells Leviathan (Job 3: 8),[82] who in the language of the Fathers signifies the devil. Rahner documents the patristic equations: *diabolus* = *draco* = Leviathan = *cetus magnus* = *aspis* (adder, asp) = *draco*.[83] St. Jerome says: "The devil surrounds the seas and the ocean on all sides."[84] The bitterness of salt-water is relevant in this connection, as it is one of the peculiarities of hell and damnation which must be fully tasted by the meditant in Loyola's *Exercises*. Point 4 of Exercise V says he must, in imagination, "taste with the taste bitter things, as tears, sadness, and the worm of conscience."[85] This is expressed even more colorfully in the *Spiritual Exercises* of the Jesuit Sebastian Izquierdo (1686): "Fourthly, the taste will be tormented with a rabid hunger and thirst, with no hope of alleviation; and its food will be bitter wormwood, and its drink water of gall."[86]

[...]

77. St. Augustine, *Expositions*, 6: 424 (Ps. 148 : 9); *PL* 36: col. 1943.

78. St. Augustine, *Expositions*, 2: 193: "Profunditas aquarum impenetrabilis."

79. Ibid., 1: 412: "Profunditas peccatorum."

80. *Homiliae in Evangelia* 2.4 (*PL* 76: col. 1116): "Aeternae mortis profunda."

81. Adam Abt, *Die Apologie des Apuleius von Madaura und die antike Zauberei* (Gießen: Alfred Töpelmann, 1908), 257 [183].

82. The Septuagint has "great whale" for Leviathan.

83. Rahner, "Antennae Crucis," 108.

84. "Diabolus maria undique circumdat et undique pontum," *Epistula II: Ad Theodosium et ceteros anachoretas intrinsecus commorantes*, in Eusebius Hieronymus [St. Jerome], *Opera*, Sect. 1, Pars 1, Epistolarum Pars 1, Corpus Scriptorum Ecclesiasticorum Latinorum, vol. 54, edited by Isidore Hilberg (Vienna: F. Tempsky; Leipzig: G. Freytag, 1910), 12.

85. "(Imaginationis) res amaras ut lachrymas, tristitiam et vermem conscientiae," *The Spiritual Exercises of St. Ignatius Loyola*, translated by Joeph Rickaby (New York: Benzinger Bros., 1922), 41.

86. "Esercizio dell'Inferno," in Sebastian Izquierdo, *Pratica di alcuni Esercizj Spirituali di S. Ignazio* (Florence: Michele Nestenus 1718), K 6. The concluding words are reminiscent of Jeremiah 23: 15: "Behold, I will feed them with wormwood, and make them drink the water of the gall."

G. *The Regeneration in Sea-Water*

After these long digressions on the interrelated symbols that branch out from the sea and its various aspects, we will resume our discussion of salt and salt-water.

The *aqua pontica* (or *aqua permanens*) behaves very much like the baptismal water of the Church. Its chief function is ablution, the cleansing of the sinner, and in alchemy this is the "lato," the impure body;[87] hence the oft-repeated saying attributed to Elbo Interfector:[88] "Whiten the lato[89] and rend the books, lest your hearts be rent asunder."[90] In the *Rosarium* the ablution[91] of the lato occurs in variant form: it is cleansed not by water but by "Azoth and fire,[92] that is, by a kind of baptism in fire, which is often used as a synonym for water.[93] The equivalent of this in the Catholic rite is the plunging of a burning candle into the font, in accordance with Matthew 3:11: "He shall baptize you with the Holy Ghost, and with fire."[94] The alchemists did not hesitate to call the transforma-

---

87. *Rosinus ad Sarrat.* (*Art. aurif.,* 1:280): "But the lato is the unclean body [*Latum autem est immundum corpus*]."

88. For instance in Maier, *Symb. aur. mensae,* 15.

89. The whitened lato is identical with the "crystalline salt" (Khunrath, *Vom Hyle-alischen,* 197.) The lato, too, is an imperfect yellow body compounded of Sun and Moon: when you have whitened it and restored it to its pristine yellowness, you have the lato again...Then you have passed through the door and have the beginning of the art." It is the *prima materia lapidis* in the state of *vilitas,* "baseness," from which the "pearl of great price" arises (Mylius, *Phil. ref.,* 199). This passage seems to be taken from *Consilium coniugii* (*Ars chemica,* 134). The lato is the "black earth" (ibid., 80, also 39). According to Du Cange, "lato" has something to do with "electrum." Cf. Edmund O. von Lippmann, *Entstehung und Ausbreitung der Alchemie* (Berlin: Julius Springer), 481.

90. Dealbate Latonem et libros rumpite, ne corda vestra corrumpantur." *Ros. phil.* (*Art. aurif.,* 2:355) cites this saying from Geber, but in corrupt form: "reponite" instead of "rumpite."

91. *Ablutio* was understood by the alchemists as *distillatio.* Cf. Mylius, *Phil. ref.,* 35.

92. Quotation from Hermes: "Azoth and fire cleanse the lato, and remove the blackness from it [*Azoth et ignis latonem abluunt, et nigredinem ab eo auferunt*]" (*Art. aurif.,* 2:277).

93. Mylius has: "Fire and water cleanse the lato and wipe off its blackness [*Ignis et aqua latonem abluunt et eius nigredinem abstergunt*]," *Phil. ref.,* 297.

94. The fire symbolism connected with baptism is expressed particularly clearly in

tive process a "baptism." Thus the *Consilium coniugii* says: "And if we are baptized in the fountain of gold and silver [*in fonte auri et argenti baptisati*], and the spirit of our body ascends into heaven with the father and the son, and descends again, then our souls shall revive and my animal body will remain white, that is, [the body] of the moon."[95] The subject of this sentence is Sol and Luna. The *Aurora consurgens I* distinguishes three kinds of baptism, "in water, in blood, and in fire,"[96] the Christian ideas being here transferred directly to the chemical procedure. The same is true of the idea that baptism is a submersion in death (following Colossians 2: 12): "(Ye are) buried with him in baptism, wherein also ye are risen with him." In his Table of Symbols, Penotus[97] correlates the "moon, the spirits and ghosts of the dead (*Manes et Lemures*), and gods of the underworld" with the "mystery of baptism," and the corresponding stage in the opus is the *solutio,* which signifies the total dissolution of the imperfect body in the *aqua divina,* its submersion, mortification,[98] and burial. The putrefaction takes place in the grave, and the foul smell that accompanies it is the stench of the graves.[99] The motif of imprisonment in the underworld is found in Greek alchemy, in the treatise of Comarius: "Lock them [the substances] in Hades."[100] The rebirth from the floods of Hades and from

---

the hymn of St. Romanus, *De theophania*: "I behold him in the midst of the floods, him who once appeared as dew in the fire in the midst of the three youths [Daniel 3: 24f.], now a fire shining in the Jordan." *Analecta sacra Spicilegio Solesmensi praeparate,* edited by Jean-Baptiste-François Pitra, 8 vols. (Paris: A. Jouby et Roger, 1876–91), 1: 21.

95. *Consil. coniug. (Ars chemica,* 128).

96. Parable 4. Another passage has: "But when he baptizes, he infuses the soul [Quando autem baptizat tunc infundit animam]." Zentralbibliothek Zurich, Codex Rhenoviensis 172.

97. *Theatr. chem.,* 2: 123.

98. The classic example of this is the dissolution of Gabricus in the body of Beya, into "atoms" (*partes indivisibiles*), *Ros. phil. (Art. aurif.,* 2: 246).

99. Morienus, *Sermo de transmutatione metallica (Art. aurif.,* 2: 33).

100. The text is in a poor state here. The passage is apparently attributed to Stephanos, and occurs not only in the treatise of Comarius (Marcellin Berthelot, *Collection des anciens alchimistes grecs* [Paris: Georges Steinheil, 1887–88], IV.xx.13, lines 17 and 20) but also in Zosimos (ibid., II.ii). Whether Stephanos (7th cent.) would have expressed himself in such an old-fashioned way is uncertain. The passage does in fact belong in the treatise of Comarius, where it also occurs in different words at 10, lines 22ff. This runs: "The waves injure them [the substances]...in Hades and in the grave

the grave recurs in Cyril of Jerusalem: "That saving flood is both your sepulchre and your mother,"[101] and in St. Augustine: "The water leads him down, as if dying, into the grave; the Holy Spirit brings him up, as if rising again, into heaven."[102]

The treatise of Ostanes[103] says that when preparing the divine water, the vessel with the ingredients should be immersed in sea-water, and then the divine water will be perfected. It is, so to speak, gestated in the womb of the sea-water. The text says: "This [divine] water makes the dead living and the living dead, it lights the darkness and darkens the light, concentrates the sea-water and quenches fire." As this miraculous water occurs even in the oldest texts, it must be of pagan rather than of Christian Origin. The oldest Chinese treatise known to us (A.D. 142) likewise contains this idea of the divine water: it is the "flowing pearl" (quicksilver), and the divine ch'i, meaning "air, spirit, ethereal essence." The various essences are likened to "spring showers in abundance,"[104] and this recalls the "blessed water" in the treatise of Komarios, which brings the spring.[105] The age-old use of water at sacrifices and the great role it played in Egypt, where Western alchemy originated, may well have foreshadowed the water symbolism of later times. Folk ideas and superstitions such as we find in the Magic Papyri may have made their contribution, too; the following words might just as well have been taken from an alchemical treatise: "I am the plant named Bai:s, I am a spout of blood, . . . the outgrowth of the abyss.[106] I am the sacred bird Phoenix[107] . . . I am Helios . . . I am

---

where they lie. But when the grave is opened, they will rise up from Hades like the newborn from the belly."

101. *Catecheses mystagogicae quinque*, II.4 (*PG* 33: col. 1080).

102. "Aqua velut morientem deducit in tumulum; spiritus sanctus velut resurgentem perducit ad caelum," *Analecta sacra*, 5: 150.

103. Berthelot, *Alch. grecs*, IV.ii.2.

104. Lu-Chiang Wu, Tenney L. Davis, and Wei Po-yang, "An Ancient Chinese Treatise on Alchemy," 238 and 251.

105. Berthelot, *Alch. grecs*, IV.xx.8, 9, 12.

106. The ἐναβύσσαιον ὕδωρ (abyssal water) is mentioned in the treatise of Christianos, "The Making of the Mystical Water" (Berthelot, *Alch. grecs*, VI.v.6, line 12).

107. Probably the earliest reference to the phoenix is in Zosimos (Berthelot, *Alch. grecs*, III.vi.5), where a quotation from Ostanes speaks of an "eagle of brass, who descends into the pure spring and bathes there every day, thus renewing himself."

Aphrodite . . . I am Kronos, who has showed forth the light . . . I am Osiris, named water, I am Isis, named dew, I am Esenephys, named spring." [108] The personified divine water might well have spoken like that.

The effect of Christian baptism is the washing away of sin and the acceptance of the neophyte into the Church as the earthly kingdom of Christ, sanctification and rebirth through grace, and the bestowal of an "indelible character" on the baptized. The effect of the *aqua permanens* is equally miraculous. The *Gloria mundi* says: "The mystery of every thing is life, which is water; for water dissolves the body into spirit and summons a spirit from the dead." [109] Dissolution into spirit, the body's volatilization or sublimation, corresponds chemically to evaporation, or any rate to the expulsion of evaporable ingredients like quicksilver, sulphur, etc. Psychologically it corresponds to the conscious realization and integration of an unconscious content. Unconscious contents lurk somewhere in the body like so many demons of sickness, impossible to get hold of, especially when they give rise to physical symptoms the organic causes of which cannot be demonstrated. The "spirit" summoned from the dead is usually the Spirit Mercurius, who, as the *anima mundi,* is inherent in all things in a latent state. It is clear from the passage immediately following that it is salt of which it is said: "And that is the thing which we seek: all our secrets are contained in it." Salt, however, "takes its origin from Mercurius," so salt is a synonym for the arcane substance. It also plays an important part in the Roman rite: after being blessed it is added to the consecrated water, and in the ceremony of baptism a few grains of the consecrated salt are placed in the neophyte's mouth with the words: "Receive the salt of wisdom: may it be a propitiation for thee unto eternal life."

As the alchemists strove to produce an incorruptible "glorified body," they would, if they were successful, attain that state in the *albedo,* where the body became spotless and no longer subject to decay. The white substance of the ash [110] was therefore described as the "diadem of the heart," and its synonym, the white foliated earth, as the "crown of victory." [111]

---

108. *Pap. Graec. Mag.,* 2: 73, XII, lines 228–38.

109. *Mus. herm.,* 262; *HM* 1: 211). This opinion is put into the mouth of "Socrates," and corresponds more or less to Sermo XVI of the *Turba.*

110. Ash is the calcined and annealed substance, freed from all decomposition.

111. *De chemia Senioris antiquissimi philosophi libellus* (Strasbourg: Samuel Emmel,

The ash is identical with the "pure water" which is "cleansed from the darkness of the soul [*tenebris animae*], and of the black matter [*materia nigredinis*], for the wickedness [*malitia*] of base earthiness [*terrestreitas mala*] has been separated from it."[112] This *terrestreitas mala* is the *terra damnata* (accursed earth) mentioned by other authors; it is what Goethe calls the "trace of earth painful to bear," the moral turpitude that cannot be washed off. In Senior, the ash is synonymous with *vitrum* (glass), which, on account of its incorruptibility and transparency, seemed to resemble the glorified body. Glass in its turn was associated with salt, for salt was praised as "that virgin and pure earth," and the "finest crystalline glass" is composed mainly of *sal Sodae* (soda salts), with sand added as a binding agent. Thus the raw material of glass-making (technically known as the "batch") is "formed from two incorruptible substances."[113] Furthermore, glass is made in the fire, the "pure" element. In the sharp or burning taste of salt the alchemists detected the fire dwelling within it, whose preservative property it in fact shares. Alexander of Macedon is cited as saying: "Know that the salt is fire and dryness."[114] Or, "the salts are of fiery nature."[115] Salt has an affinity with sulphur, whose nature is essentially fiery.[116] Glauber maintains that "fire and salt are in their essential nature one thing" and are therefore "held in high esteem by all sensible Christians, but the ignorant know no more of these things than a cow, a pig, or a brute, which live without understanding." He also says the "Abyssinians" baptized with water and fire. Without fire and salt the

---

c.1560), 41: "The white foliated earth is the crown of victory, which is ash extracted from ash, and their second body [*Terra alba foliata est Corona victoriae, quae est cinis extractus a cinere, & corpus eorum secundum*]." The connection with 1 Thess. 2: 19, "... our hope, or joy, or crown of glory" (DV), is doubtful, likewise with Isaiah 28: 5, "...the Lord of hosts shall by a crown of glory" (DV). On the other hand, Isaiah 61: 3, "...to give them a crown for ashes," is of importance for the alchemical connection between ashes, diadem, and crown. Cf. Erwin R. Goodenough, "The Crown of Victory in Judaism," *The Art Bulletin* 28, no. 3 (September 1946): 139–59.

112. *De chemia Senioris,* 40.

113. *De igne & sale* (*Theatr. chem.,* 6: 44f.).

114. *Mus. herm.,* 217; *HM* 1: 176.

115. *De igne & sale* (*Theatr. chem.,* 6: 57).

116. *Mus. herm.,* 217; *HM* 1: 176.

heathen would not have been able to offer sacrifice, and the evangelist Mark had said that "every one shall be salted with fire, and every sacrifice shall be salted with salt."[117]

H. *The Interpretation and Meaning of Salt*

Salt as much as ash is a synonym for the *albedo* (or *dealbatio*), and is identical with "the white stone, the white sun, the full moon, the fruitful white earth, cleansed and calcined."[118] The connecting link between ash and salt is potash, and the burning and corrosive property of lye (caustic solution) is well known.[119] Senior mentions that the *dealbatio* was known as "salsatura" (marination).[120]

Some light is thrown on the numerous overlapping significations of salt, and the obscurity begins to clear up, when we are informed, further, that one of its principal meanings is *soul*. As the white substance it is the "white woman," and the "salt of our magnesia"[121] is a "spark of the *anima mundi*."[122] For Glauber, salt is feminine and corresponds to Eve.[123] The *Gloria mundi* says: "The salt of the earth is the soul."[124] This pregnant sentence contains within it the whole ambiguity of alchemy. On the one hand, the soul is the "*aqua permanens,* which dissolves and coagulates," the arcane substance which is at once the transformer and the transformed, the nature which conquers nature. On the other hand, it is the human soul imprisoned in the body as the *anima mundi* is in matter, and this soul undergoes the same transformations by death and purification,

---

117. Glauber, *Tract. de natura salium,* 16f. Glauber alludes here to Mark 9:49.

118. "Lapis albus, sol albus, Luna plena, terra alba fructuosa, mundificata et calcinata," Mylius, *Phil. ref.,* 20.

119. Cf. the *Liber de aluminibus et salibus,* attributed to Rhasis or to Garlandus (*Buch der Alaune und Salze: Ein Grundwerk der spätlateinischen Alchemie,* edited by Julius Ruska (Berlin: Verlag Chemie, 1935 [1905]), 81 ff.). This purely chemical treatise of Arabic origin gives some idea of what the early medieval alchemists knew of chemistry.

120. *De chemia Senioris,* 42.

121. For the alchemists, magnesia was as a rule an arcane substance and not a specifically chemical one. Cf. *CW* 9.2: *Aion,* pars. 241f., 244.

122. Khunrath, *Vom Hylealischen,* 197.

123. Glauber, *Tract. de signatura salium,* 12. For Eve as the feminine element contained in the man, see "Psychology and Religion," par. 47, n. 22.

124. *Mus. herm.,* 217; *HM* 1:176: "Sal terrae est anima."

and finally by glorification, as the lapis. It is the tincture which "coagulates" all substances, indeed it even "fixes" (*figit*) itself; it comes "from the center of the earth and is the destroyed earth, nor is there anything on the earth like to the tincture."[125] The soul is therefore not an earthly but a transcendental thing, regardless of the fact that the alchemists expected it to appear in a retort. This contradiction presented no difficulties to the medieval mind. There was a good reason for this: the philosophers were so fascinated by their own psychisms that, in their naivete, they faithfully reproduced the inner psychic situation externally. Although the unconscious, personified by the anima, is in itself transcendental, it can appear in the sphere of consciousness, that is, in this world, in the form of an "influence" on conscious processes.

Just as the world-soul pervades all things, so does salt. It is ubiquitous and thus fulfills the main requirement of an arcane substance, that it can be found everywhere. No doubt the reader will be as conscious as I am of how uncommonly difficult it is to give an account of salt and its ubiquitous connections. It represents the feminine principle of Eros, which brings everything into relationship, in an almost perfect way. In this respect it is surpassed only by Mercurius, and the notion that salt comes from Mercurius is therefore quite understandable. For salt, as the soul or spark of the anima mundi, is in very truth the daughter of the spiritus vegetativus of creation. Salt is far more indefinite and more universal than sulphur, whose essence is fairly well defined by its fiery nature.

The relationship of salt to the anima mundi, which as we know is personified by the Primordial Man or Anthropos, brings us to the analogy with Christ. Glauber himself makes the equation Sal: Sol= A : Ω ,[126] so that salt becomes an analogue of God. According to Glauber, the sign for salt $\ominus$ was originally $\unicode{x25D1}$,[127] a double totality symbol; the circle representing non-differentiated wholeness, and the square discriminated

125. Ibid., 218. How very much the tincture is the "baptismal water" can be seen from the Greek (Berthelot, *Alch. grecs,* VI.xviii.4, line 2): "Being bodies they become spirits, so that he will baptize in the tincture of the spirit." There is a similar passage in Pelagios (Berthelot, *Alch. grecs,* IV.i.9, lines 17ff.). We are reminded of the famous passage about the krater in Zosimos (Berthelot, *Alch. grecs,* III.li, line 8): "baptized in the *krater,*" referring to the baptism of Theosebeia into the Poimandres community.

126. Glauber, *Tract. de signatura salium,* 15.

127. Ibid., 23

wholeness. As a matter of fact there is another sign for salt, ♇ in contra-distinction to ♀ Venus, who certainly has less to do with understanding and wisdom than has salt. Salt, says Glauber, was the "first fiat" at the creation.[128] Christ is the salt of wisdom which is given at babtism.[129] These ideas are elaborated by Georg von Welling: Christ is the salt, the fiat is the Word that is begotten from eternity for our preservation. Christ is the "sweet, fixed salt of silent, gentle eternity." The body, when salted by Christ, becomes tinctured and therefore incorruptible.[130]

The Christ parallel runs through the late alchemical speculations that set in after Boehme, and it was made possible by the *sal*: *sapientia* equation. Already in antiquity salt denoted wit, good sense, good taste, etc., as well as spirit. Cicero, for instance, remarks: "In wit [sale] and humour Caesar...surpassed them all."[131] But it was the Vulgate that had the most decisive influence on the formation of alchemical concepts. In the Old Testament, even the "salt of the covenant"[132] has a moral meaning. In the New Testament, the famous words "Ye are the salt of the earth" (Matthew 5: 13) show that the disciples were regarded as personifications of higher insight and divine wisdom, just as, in their role of ἀπόστολοι (proclaimers of the message), they functioned as "angels" (ἄγγελοι, "messengers"), so that God's kingdom on earth might approximate as closely as possible to the structure of the heavenly hierarchy. The other well-known passage is at Mark 9: 50, ending with the words: "Have salt in yourselves, and have peace one with another." The earliest reference to salt in the New Testament (Colossians 4: 6) likewise has a classical flavor: "Let your speech be always with grace, and seasoned with salt, that ye may know how ye ought to answer every man."

Here salt undoubtedly means insight, understanding, wisdom. In both Matthew and Mark the salt is liable to lose its savor. Evidently this salt must keep its tang, just as the wise virgins kept their lamps trimmed.

---

128. Glauber, *Tract. de natura salium*, 44.

129. Ibid., 51.

130. Von Welling, *Opus Mago-Cabbalisticum*, 6 and 31.

131. "Sale vero et facetiis Caesar...vicit omnes," *De officiis* 1.133. Cicero, *On Duties*, translated by Walter Miller, Loeb Classical Library 30 (Cambridge, Mass.: Harvard University Press, 1913), 136f.

132. For instance, Leviticus 2: 13.

For this purpose a flexibility of mind is needed, and the last thing to guarantee this is rigid insistence on the necessity of faith. Everyone will admit that it is the task of the Church to safeguard her store of wisdom, the *aqua doctrinae,* in its original purity, and yet, in response to the changing spirit of the times, she must go on altering it and differentiating it just as the Fathers did. For the cultured Greco-Roman world early Christianity was among other things a message in philosophical disguise, as we can see quite plainly from Hippolytus. It was a competing philosophical doctrine that reached a certain peak of perfection in St. Thomas. Until well into the sixteenth century the degree of philosophical truth of Christian doctrine corresponded to that of scientific truth today.

The physicians and natural philosophers of the Middle Ages nevertheless found themselves faced with problems for which the Church had no answer. Confronted with sickness and death, the physicians did not hesitate to seek counsel with the Arabs and so resuscitate that bit of the ancient world which the Church thought she had exterminated forever, namely the Mandaean and Sabaean remnants of Hellenistic syncretism. From them they derived a *sal sapientiae* that seemed so unlike the doctrine of the Church that before long a process of mutual assimilation arose which put forth some very remarkable blossoms. The ecclesiastical allegories kept, so far as I can judge, to the classical usage of *Sal.* Only St. Hilary (d. 367) seems to have gone rather more deeply into the nature of salt when he remarks that "salt contains in itself the element of water and fire, and by this is one out of two."[133] Picinellus observes: "Two elements that stir up an implacable enmity between themselves are found in wondrous alliance in salt. For salt is wholly fire and wholly water [*Sal enim simul totus est ignis, & totus aqua*]."[134] For the rest he advises a sparing use of salt: "Let the word be sprinkled with [salt], not deluged with it,"[135] and another, earlier allegorist, the Jesuit Nicolas Caussin,[136] does not mention salt at all.

---

133. "Sal est in se uno continens aquae et ignis elementum; et hoc ex duobus est unum," *Commentarium in Matthaei Evangelium* 4.10 (*PL* 9: col. 954).

134. Philippus Picinellus (Filippo Picinello), *Mundus symbolicus,* 2 vols. (Cologne: Hermann Demen, 1687), 1: 711.

135. "Aspergatur sermo sapientia, non obruatur," ibid., 1: 712.

136. *Polyhistor symbolicus* (Paris: Roman de Beauvais, 1618).

This is not altogether surprising, for how do wisdom and revelation square with one another? As certain books of the Old Testament canon show, there is, besides the wisdom of God which expresses itself in revelation, a human wisdom which cannot be had unless one works for it. Mark 9: 50 therefore exhorts us to make sure that we always have enough salt in us, and he is certainly not referring to divine revelation, for this is something no man can produce on his own resources. But at least he can cultivate and increase his own human wisdom. That Mark should offer this warning, and that Paul should express himself in a very similar way, is in accord with the traditional Judeo-Hellenism of the Jewish communities at that time. An authoritarian Church, however, leaves very little room for the salt of human wisdom. Hence it is not surprising that the *sal sapientiae* plays an incomparably greater role outside the Church. Irenaeus, reporting the views of the Gnostics, says: "The spiritual, they say, [is] sent forth to this end, that, being united here below with the psychic, it may take form, and be instructed simultaneously by intercourse with it. And this they declare to be 'the salt' and 'the light of the world.'"[137] The union of the spiritual, masculine principle with the feminine, psychic principle is far from being just a fantasy of the Gnostics: it has found an echo in the Assumption of the Virgin, in the union of Tifereth and Malchuth, and in Goethe's "the Eternal Feminine leads us upward and on." Hippolytus mentions this same view as that of the Sethians. He says:

> But when this wave is raised from the water by the wind and made pregnant in its nature, and has received within itself the reproductive power of the feminine, it retains the light scattered from on high together with the fragrance of the spirit [πνεύματος],[138] and that is Nous given shape in various forms. This [light] is a perfect God, who is brought down from the unbegotten light on high and from the spirit into man's nature as into a temple, by the power of nature and the movement of the wind. It is engendered from the water and commingled and mixed with the bodies as if it were the salt of all created things, and a light of the darkness struggling to be freed from the bodies, and not able to find a way out. For some very small spark

---

137. Irenaeus, *Adversus haereses* i.vi.i. Cf. *The Writings of Irenaeus*, translated by Alexander Roberts and W. H. Rambaut, 2 vols. (Edinburgh: T. & T. Clark, 1868–69), 25.

138. Here *pneuma* has the meaning of a holy spirit and not of wind.

of the light is mingled with the fragrance from above … [Here follows a corrupt and controversial passage, which I pass over.] Therefore every thought and care of the light from above is how and in what way the Nous may be delivered from the death of the sinful and dark body, from the father below [τοῦ κάτωθεν],[139] who is the wind which raised up the waves in tumult and terror, and begot Nous his own perfect son, who is yet not his own son in substance. For he was a ray of light from on high, from that perfect light overpowered in the dark and terrible, bitter polluted water, and a shining spirit carried away over the water.[140]

This strangely beautiful passage contains pretty well everything that the alchemists endeavored to say about salt: it is the spirit, the turning of the body into light (*albedo*), the spark of the *anima mundi,* imprisoned in the dark depths of the sea and begotten there by the light from above and the "reproductive power of the feminine." It should be noted that the alchemists could have known nothing of Hippolytus, as his *Philosophumena,* long believed lost, was rediscovered only in the middle of the nineteenth century in a monastery on Mount Athas. Anyone familiar with the spirit of alchemy and the views of the Gnostics in Hippolytus will be struck again and again by their inner affinity.

The clue to this passage from the *Elenchos,* and to other similar ones, is to be found in the phenomenology of the self.[141] Salt is not a very common dream-symbol, but it does appear in the cubic form of a crystal,[142] which in many patients' drawings represents the center and hence the self; similarly, the quaternary structure of most mandalas reminds one of the sign for salt ⊕ mentioned earlier. Just as the numerous synonyms and attributes of the lapis stress now one and now another of its aspects, so do the symbols of the self. Apart from its preservative quality salt has

---

139. "Death" and the "father below" are both preceded by the same ἀπό (from) and are therefore parallel if not identical, insofar as the begetter of life is also the begetter of death. This is an indication of the ineluctable polaristic nature of the *auctor rerum.*

140. *Philosophumena or The Refutation of All Heresies,* translated by F. Legge, 2 vols. (London: Society for Promoting Christian Knowledge; New York: Macmillan, 1921), 1: 163f. [translation modified].

141. See *CW* 9.2: *Aion,* ch. 13.

142. Cubic salt crystals are mentioned in Von Welling, *Opus Mago-Cabbalisticum,* 41.

mainly the metaphorical meaning of *sapientia*. With regard to this aspect the *Tractatus aureus* states:

> It is said in the mystic language of our sages, He who works without salt will never raise dead bodies...He who works without salt draws a bow without a string. For you must know that these sayings refer to a very different kind of salt from the common mineral...Sometimes they call the medicine itself "Salt."[143]

These words are ambiguous: here salt means "wit" as well as wisdom. As to the importance of salt in the opus, Johannes Grasseus says of the arcane substance: "And this is the Lead of the Philosophers which they also call the lead of the air. In it is found the shining white dove, named the salt of the metals, wherein is the whole magistery of the work. This [dove] is the pure, chaste, wise, and rich Queen of Sheba[144] Here salt, arcane substance (the paradoxical "lead of the air"), the white dove (*spiritus sapientiae*), wisdom, and femininity appear in one figure. The saying from the *Gloria mundi* is quite clear: "No man can understand this Art who does not know the salt and its preparation."[145] For the "Aquarium sapientum" the *sal sapientiae* comes from the *aqua benedicta* or *aqua pontica*, which, itself an extract, is named "heart, soul, and spirit." At first the *aqua* is contained in the *prima materia* and is "of a blood-red color; but after its preparation it becomes of a bright, clear, transparent white, and is called by the sages the Salt of Wisdom."[146] Khunrath boldly summarizes these statements about the salt when he says: "Our water cannot be made without the salt of wisdom, for it is the salt of wisdom itself, say the philosophers; a fire, and a salt fire, the true Living Universal Menstruum." "Without salt the work has no success."[147] Elsewhere he remarks: "Not without good reason has salt been adorned by the wise with the name of Wisdom." Salt is the lapis, a "mystery to be hidden."[148] Vigenerus says that the Redeemer chose his disciples "that they might be the salt of men and proclaim to them the pure and incorruptible doctrine of the gospel." He reports the "Cabalists"

---

143. *Mus. herm.*, 20; *HM* 1: 22.
144. *Arca arcani* (*Theatr. chem.*, 6: 314).
145. *Mus. herm.*, 216; *HM* 1: 176.
146. *Mus. herm.*, 88; *HM* 1: 80.
147. Khunrath, *Vom Hylealischen*, 229, 254.
148. Khunrath, *Amphitheatrum*, 197. The lapis, however, corresponds to the self.

as saying that the "computatio"[149] of the Hebrew word for salt (*melach*) gives the number 78. This number could be divided by any divisor and still give a word that referred to the divine Name. We will not pursue the inferences he draws from this but will only note that for all those reasons salt was used "for the service of God in all offerings and sacrifices."[150] Glauber calls Christ the sal sapientiae and says that his favorite disciple John was "salted with the salt of wisdom."[151]

Apart from its lunar wetness and its terrestrial nature, the most outstanding properties of salt are bitterness and wisdom. As in the double quaternio of the elements and qualities, earth and water have coldness in common, so bitterness and wisdom would form a pair of opposites with a third thing between. (See diagram below.) The factor common to both, however incommensurable the two ideas may seem, is, psychologically, the function of feeling. Tears, sorrow, and disappointment are bitter, but wisdom is the comforter in all psychic suffering. Indeed, bitterness and wisdom form a pair of alternatives: where there is bitterness wisdom is lacking, and where wisdom is there can be no bitterness. Salt, as the carrier of this fateful alternative, is coordinated with the nature of woman.

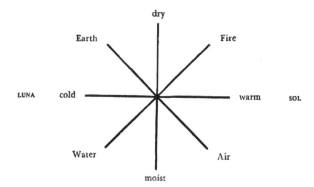

---

149. By "computatio" is meant the "isopsephia," that is, the sum that results from the numerical values of the letters in a word, this word being then equated with another word having the same numerical value.

150. *De igne & sale* (*Theatr. chem.*, 6: 129f.).

151. Glauber, *Tract. de natura salium,* 25 and 51. Christ as *sal sapientiae* is another symbol of the self.

The masculine, solar nature in the right half of the quaternio knows neither coldness, nor a shadow, nor heaviness, melancholy, etc., because, so long as all goes well, it identifies as closely as possible with consciousness, and that as a rule is the idea which one has of oneself. In this idea the shadow is usually missing: first because nobody likes to admit to any inferiority, and second because logic forbids something white to be called black. A good man has good qualities, and only the bad man has bad qualities. For reasons of prestige we pass over the shadow in complete silence. A famous example of masculine prejudice is Nietzsche's Superman, who scorns compassion and fights against the "Ugliest Man"—the ordinary man that everyone is. The shadow must not be seen, it must be denied, repressed, or twisted into something quite extraordinary. The sun is always shining and everything smiles back. There is no room for any prestige-diminishing weakness, so the *sol niger* is never seen. Only in solitary hours is its presence feared.

Things are different with Luna: every month she is darkened and extinguished; she cannot hide this from anybody, not even from herself. She knows that this same Luna is now bright and now dark—but who has ever heard of a dark sun? We call this quality of Luna "woman's closeness to nature," and the fiery brilliance and hot air that plays round the surface of things we like to call "the masculine mind."

Despite all attempts at denial and obfuscation there is an unconscious factor, a black sun, which is responsible for the surprisingly common phenomenon of masculine split-mindedness, when the right hand mustn't know what the left is doing. This split in the masculine psyche and the regular darkening of the moon in woman together explain the remarkable fact that the woman is accused of all the darkness in a man, while he himself basks in the thought that he is a veritable fount of vitality and illumination for all the females in his environment. Actually, he would be better advised to shroud the brilliance of his mind in the profoundest doubt. It is not difficult for this type of mind (which besides other things is a great trickster like Mercurius) to admit a host of sins in the most convincing way, and even to combine it with a spurious feeling of ethical superiority without in the least approximating to a genuine insight. This can never be achieved without the participation of feeling; but the intellect admits feeling only when it is convenient. The novilunium of woman is a source of countless disappointments for man which easily turn to bitterness, though they could equally well be a source of wisdom if they were understood. Naturally this is possible only if he is prepared to acknowledge his black sun, that is, his shadow.

Confirmation of our interpretation of salt as Eros (i.e., as a feeling relationship) is found in the fact that the bitterness is the origin of the *colors.* We have only to look at the drawings and paintings of patients who supplement their analysis by active imagination to see that colors are feeling-values. Mostly, to begin with, only a pencil or pen is used to make rapid sketches of dreams, sudden ideas, and fantasies. But from a certain moment on the patients begin to make use of color, and this is generally the moment when merely intellectual interest gives way to emotional participation. Occasionally the same phenomenon can be observed in dreams, which at such moments are dreamt in color, or a particularly vivid color is insisted upon.

Disappointment, always a shock to the feelings, is not only the mother of bitterness but the strongest incentive to a differentiation of feeling. The failure of a pet plan, the disappointing behavior of someone one loves, can supply the impulse either for a more or less brutal outburst of affect or for a modification and adjustment of feeling, and hence for its higher development. This culminates in wisdom if feeling is supplemented by reflection and rational insight. Wisdom is never violent: where wisdom reigns there is no conflict between thinking and feeling.

This interpretation of salt and its qualities prompts us to ask, as in all cases where alchemical statements are involved, whether the alchemists themselves had such thoughts. We know from the literature that they were thoroughly aware of the moral meaning of the *amaritudo,* and by *sapientia* they did not mean anything essentially different from what we understand by this word. But how the wisdom comes from the bitterness, and how the bitterness can be the source of the colors, on these points they leave us in the dark. Nor have we any reason to believe that these connections were so self-evident to them that they regarded any explanation as superfluous. If that were so, someone would have been sure to blurt it out. It is much more probable that they simply said these things without any conscious act of cognition. Moreover, the sum of all these statements is seldom or never found consistently formulated in any one author; rather one author mentions one thing and another another, and it is only by viewing them all together, as we have tried to do here, that we get the whole picture.[152] The alchemists themselves suggest this method, and I must admit that it was their advice which first put me on the track of a psychological interpretation. The *Rosarium* says one should "read from page to page," and other sayings are "He should possess many books" and "One book opens another." Yet the complete lack, until the nineteenth century, of any psychological viewpoint (which even today meets with the grossest misunderstandings) makes it very unlikely that anything resembling a psychological interpretation penetrated into the consciousness of the alchemists. Their moral concepts moved entirely on the plane of synonym and analogy, in a word, of "correspondence." Most of their statements spring not from a conscious but from an unconscious act of thinking, as do dreams, sudden ideas, and fantasies, where again we only find out the meaning afterwards by careful comparison and analysis.

But the greatest of all riddles, of course, is the ever-recurring question of what the alchemists really meant by their substances. What, for instance, is the meaning of a "sal spirituale?" The only possible answer seems to be this: chemical matter was so completely unknown to them that it instantly became a carrier for projections. Its darkness was so loaded with unconscious contents that a state of *participation mystique*,[153]

---

152. Olympiodorus (Berthelot, *Alch. grecs*, II.iv.38) remarks: "Thus the key to the meaning of the circular art is the synopsis thereof." And the *Turba* says: "The more I read the books, the more I am enlightened [*Quanto magis libros legebam, tanto magis mihi illuminabatur*]," Ruska, *Turba Philosophorum*, 125 (Sermo XV).

153. I take the concept of *participation mystique*, in the sense defined above, from the works of [Lucien] Lévy-Bruhl. Recently, this idea has been repudiated by ethnologists, partly for the reason that primitives know very well how to differentiate between things. There is no doubt about that; but it cannot be denied, either, that incommensurable things can have, for them, an equally incommensurable *tertium comparationis*. One has only to think of the ubiquitous application of "mana," the werewolf motif, etc. Furthermore, "unconscious identity" is a psychic phenomenon which the psychotherapist has to deal with every day. Certain ethnologists have also rejected Lévy-Bruhl's concept of the *état prélogique*, which closely connected with that of *participation*. The term is not a very happy one, for in his own way the primitive thinks just as logically as we do. Lévy-Bruhl was aware of this, as I know from personal conversation with

or unconscious identity, arose between them and the chemical substance, which caused this substance to behave, at any rate in part, like an unconscious content. Of this relationship the alchemists had a dim presentiment-enough, anyway, to enable them to make statements that can only be understood as psychological.

Khunrath says: "And the Light was made Salt, a body of salt, the salt of wisdom." [154] The same author remarks that the "point in the midst of the salt" corresponds to the "Tartarus of the greater world," which is hell. [155] This coincides with the conception of the fire hidden in the salt. Salt must have the paradoxical double nature of the arcane substance. Thus the *Gloria mundi* says that "in the salt are two salts," namely sulphur and the "radical moisture," the two most potent opposites imaginable, for which reason it was also called the Rebis. [156] Vigenerus asserts that salt consists of two substances, since all salts partake of sulphur and quicksilver. [157] These correspond to Khunrath's "king and queen," the two "waters, red and white." [158] During the work the salt "assumes the appearance of blood." [159] "It is certain," says Dorn, "that a salt, the natural balsam of the body, is begotten from human blood. It has within it both corruption and preservation against corruption, for in the natural order there is nothing that does not contain as much evil as good." [160] Dorn was a physician, and his remark is characteristic of the empirical standpoint of the alchemists.

---

him. By "prelogical" he meant the primitive presuppositions that contradict only our rationalistic logic. These presuppositions are often exceedingly strange, and though they may not deserve to be called "prelogical" they certainly merit the term irrational." Astonishingly enough Lévy-Bruhl, in his posthumously published diary, recanted both these concepts. This is the more remarkable in that they had a thoroughly sound psychological basis.

154. Khunrath, *Vom Hylealischen*, 74. Probably an allusion to John 1: 9: "That was the true Light, which lighteth," etc.

155. Ibid., 194

156. *Mus. herm.*, 217f.; *HM* 1: 177.

157. *Theatr. chem.*, 6: 127.

158. Khunrath, *Vom Hylealischen*, 197f.

159. *Mus. herm.*, 216.

160. Gerhard Dorn, *Speculative philosophiae* (*Theatr. chem.*, 1: 307).

The dark nature of salt accounts for its "blackness and foetid smell."[161] At the dissolution of living bodies it is the "last residue of corruption, [*ultimum in corruptione*]" but it is the "prime agent in generation [*primum in generatione*]."[162] Mylius expressly identifies salt with the uroboros-dragon.[163] We have already mentioned its identification with the sea of Typhon; hence one could easily identify it with the sea-monster Leviathan.[164] At all events there is an amusing relationship between salt and the Leviathan in Abraham Eleazar, who says with reference to Job 40:15: "For Behemoth is a wild ox, whom the Most High has salted up with Leviathan and preserved for the world to come,"[165] evidently as food for the inhabitants of paradise,[166] or whatever the "world to come" may mean.

Another direful aspect of salt is its relation to the malefic Saturn, as is implied by Grasseus in that passage about the white dove and the philosophical lead. Speaking of the identity of sea and salt, Vigenerus points out that the Pythagoreans called the sea the "tear of Kronos," because of

---

161. *Mus. herm.*, 216.

162. Johann Christoph Steeb, *Coelum sephiroticum, Hebraeorum* (Mainz: Ludovico Bourgeat 1679), 26 and 29.

163. Mylius, *Phil. ref.*, 195.

164. I cannot recall ever having come across this association in the texts.

165. *Uraltes Chymisches Werck*, 2 vols. (Erfurt: Augustin Crusius, 1735), 2: 62. This story is told in abbreviated form in "Baba Bathra," translated by Israel W. Slotki, in *The Babylonian Talmud*, edited by Rabbi I. Epstein, 35 vols. (London: The Soncino Press, 1935–52), 3: 296f. (74*b*): "All that the Holy One, blessed be He, created in this world, He created male and female. Likewise, Leviathan the slant serpent and Leviathan the tortuous serpent He created male and female; and had they mated with one another they would have destroyed the whole world. What then did the Holy One, blessed be He, do? He castrated the male and killed the female, preserving it in salt for the righteous in the world to come; for it is written: And he will slay the dragon that is in the sea." He is also said to have done the same thing to Behemoth. By way of explanation I should like to add that the two prehistoric animals, Leviathan (water) and Behemoth (land), together with their females, form a quaternio of opposites. The *coniunctio oppositorum* on the animal level, i.e., in the unconscious state, is prevented by God as being dangerous, for it would keep consciousness on the animal level and hinder its further development. (Cf. *CW* 9.2: *Aion*, pars. 118f.) Regarding the connection between salt and the female element, it is significant that it was the female Leviathan that was salted.

166. According to an old tradition God, after the Fall, moved Paradise and placed it in the future.

its "bitter saltness."[167] On account of its relation to Typhon, salt is also endowed with a murderous quality,[168] as we saw in the chapter on Sulphur, where Sal inflicts on Sulphur an "incurable wound." This offers a curious parallel to Kundry' s wounding of Amfortas in *Parsifal.* In the parable of Sulphur Sal plays the sinister new-moon role of Luna.

As a natural product, salt "contains as much evil as good." As the sea it is παμμήτηρ, "mother of all things"; as the tear of Kronos it is bitterness and sadness; as the "sea-spume" it is the scum of Typhon, and as the "clear water" it is Sapientia herself.

The *Gloria mundi* says that the *aqua permanens* is a "very limpid water, so bitter as to be quite undrinkable."[169] In a hymn-like invocation the text continues: "O water of bitter taste, that preservest the elements! O nature of propinquity, that dissolvest nature! O best of natures, which overcomest nature herself!...Thou art crowned with light and art born...and the quintessence ariseth from thee."[170] This water is like none on earth, with the exception of that "fount in Judaea" which is named the "Fount of the Savior or of Blessedness." "With great efforts and by the grace of God the philosophers found that noble spring." But the spring is in a place so secret that only a few know of its "gushing," and they know not the way to Judaea where it might be found. Therefore the philosopher[171] cries out: "O water of harsh and bitter taste! For it is hard and difficult for any man to find that spring."[172] This is an obvious allusion to the arcane nature and moral significance of the water, and it is also evident that it is not the water of grace or the water of the doctrine but that

---

167. Cf. Plutarch, "Isis and Osiris," 8off.: "The saying of the Pythagoreans, that the sea is a tear of Kronos."

168. Cf. the Gnostic view that Kronos is "a power of the color of water, and alldestructive," *Philosophumena*, 154 [translation modified]). For further associations of the "bright" water, see "The Spirit Mercurius," par. 274.

169. *Mus herm.*, 222; *HM* 1: 180.

170. "O aquam in acerba specie, quae tu elementa conservas!...," ibid., 213; *HM* 1: 73.

171. Morienus, in whose treatise (*De transmutations metallica*) is found only the expression "blessed water," then the idea of the "one fount" of the four qualities, and finally, the important remark that no one attains the completion of the work "save by the affliction of the soul" (*Art. aurif.*, 2: 18, 26, 34).

172. "O aquam in amara acerbaque specie! Durum enim dificileque cui vis, ut fontem illum inveniat," *Mus. herm.*, 214; *HM* 1: 174.

it springs from the *lumen naturae*. Otherwise the author would not have emphasized that Judaea was in a "secret place," for if the Church's teachings were meant no one would need to find them in a secret place since they are accessible to everyone. Also, it would be quite incomprehensible why the philosopher should exclaim: "O water, held worthless by all! By reason of its worthlessness and tortuousness [173] no one can attain perfection in the art, or perceive its mighty virtue; for all four elements are, as it were, contained in it." There can be no doubt that this is the *aqua permanens* or *aqua pontica,* the primal water which contains the four elements.

The psychological equivalent of the chaotic water of the beginning [174] is the unconscious, which the old writers could grasp only in projected form, just as today most people cannot see the beam in their own eye but are all too well aware of the mote in their brother's. Political propaganda exploits this primitivity and conquers the naive with their own defect. The only defense against this overwhelming danger is recognition of the shadow. The sight of its darkness is itself an illumination, a widening of consciousness through integration of the hitherto unconscious components of the personality. Freud's efforts to bring the shadow to consciousness are the logical and salutary answer to the almost universal unconsciousness and projection-proneness of the general public. It is as though Freud, with sure instinct, had sought to avert the danger of nation-wide psychic epidemics that threatened Europe. What he did not see was that the confrontation with the shadow is not just a harmless affair that can be settled by "reason." The shadow is the primitive who is still alive and active in civilized man, and our civilized reason means nothing to him. He needs to be ruled by a higher authority, such as is found in the great religions. Even when Reason triumphed at the beginning of the French Revolution it was quickly turned into a goddess and enthroned in Notre-Dame.

The shadow exerts a dangerous fascination which can be countered only by another *fascinosum.* It cannot be got at by reason, even in the most

---

173. *Curvitatem,* presumably an allusion to the winding course of water and the *rivuli* (streams) of the Mercurial serpent.

174. "Darkness there was: at first concealed in darkness this All was undiscriminated chaos," *Rigveda* 10.129.2 (*Hymns of the Rigveda,* translated by Ralph T. H. Griffith, 2 vols. [Benaaes: E. J. Lazarus, 1897, 2: 575).

rational person, but only by illumination, of a degree and kind that are equal to the darkness but are the exact opposite of "enlightenment. For what we call "rational" is everything that seems "fitting" to the man in the street, and the question then arises whether this "fitness" may not in the end prove to be "irrational" in the bad sense of the word. Sometimes, even with the best intentions this dilemma cannot be solved. This is the moment when the primitive trusts himself to a higher authority and to a decision beyond his comprehension. The civilized man in his closed-in environment functions in a fitting and appropriate manner, that is, rationally. But if, because of some apparently insoluble dilemma, he gets outside the confines of civilization, he becomes a primitive again; then he has irrational ideas and acts on hunches; then he no longer thinks but "it" thinks in him; then he needs "magical" practices in order to gain a feeling of security; then the latent autonomy of the unconscious becomes active and begins to manifest itself as it has always done in the past.

The good tidings announced by alchemy are that, as once a fountain sprang up in judaea, so now there is a secret judaea the way to which is not easily found, and a hidden spring whose waters seem so worthless[175] and so bitter that they are deemed of no use at all. We know from numerous hints[176] that man's inner life is the "secret place" where the *aqua solvens et coagulans,* the *medicina catholica* or panacea, the spark of the light of nature,[177] are to be found. Our text shows us how much the alchemists put their art on the level of divine revelation and regarded it as at least an essential complement to the work of redemption. True, only a few of them were the elect who formed the golden chain linking earth to heaven, but still they were the fathers of natural science today. They were the unwitting instigators of the schism between faith and knowledge, and it was they who made the world conscious that the revelation was neither complete nor final. "Since these things are so," says an ecclesiastic of the seventeenth century, "it will suffice, after the light of faith, for human ingenuity to recognize, as it were, the refracted rays of the Divine majesty

---

175. Vilitas" was also something Christ was reproached with. Cf. John 1:46: "Can there any good thing come out of Nazareth?"

176. Cf. *CW*12: *Psychology and Alchemy,* par. 300.

177. Or as Morienus (*Art. aurif.,* 2:32) so graphically says: "Until it begins to shine like fishes' eyes."

in the world and in created things."[178] The "refracted rays" correspond to the "certain luminosity," which the alchemists said was inherent in the natural world.

Revelation conveys general truths that often do not illuminate the individual's actual situation in the slightest, nor was it traditional revelation that gave us the microscope and the machine. And since human life is not enacted exclusively, or even to a noticeable degree, on the plane of the higher verities, the source of knowledge unlocked by the old alchemists and physicians has done humanity a great and welcome service—so great that for many people the light of revelation has been extinguished altogether. Within the confines of civilization man's willful rationality apparently suffices. Outside of this shines, or should shine, the light of faith. But where the darkness comprehendeth it not (this being the prerogative of darkness!) those laboring in the darkness must try to accomplish an opus that will cause the "fishes' eyes" to shine in the depths of the sea, or to catch the "refracted rays of the divine majesty" even though this produces a light which the darkness, as usual, does not comprehend. But when there is a light in the darkness which comprehends the darkness, darkness no longer prevails. The longing of the darkness for light is fulfilled only when the light can no longer be rationally explained by the darkness. For the darkness has its own peculiar intellect and its own logic, which should be taken very seriously. Only the "light which the darkness comprehendeth not" can illuminate the darkness. Everything that the darkness thinks, grasps, and comprehends by itself is dark; therefore it is illuminated only by what, to it, is unexpected, unwanted, and incomprehensible. The psychotherapeutic method of active imagination offers excellent examples of this; sometimes a numinous dream or some external event will have the same effect.

Alchemy announced a source of knowledge, parallel if not equivalent to revelation, which yields a "bitter" water by no means acceptable to our human judgment. It is harsh and bitter or like vinegar,[179] for it is a bitter

178. "Quae cum ita sint, satis erit humano ingenio post lucem fidei, Divinae maiestatis veluti refractos in mundo, et rebus creatis agnoscere." Caussin, *Polykistor symbolicus*, 3.

179. Maier (*Symb. aur. mensae*, 568): "There is in our chemistry a certain noble

thing to accept the darkness and blackness of the *umbra solis* and to pass through this valley of the shadow. It is bitter indeed to discover behind one's lofty ideals narrow, fanatical convictions, all the more cherished for that, and behind one's heroic pretensions nothing but crude egotism, infantile greed, and complacency. This painful corrective is an unavoidable stage in every psychotherapeutic process. As the alchemists said, it begins with the *nigredo,* or generates it as the indispensable prerequisite for synthesis, for unless the opposites are constellated and brought to consciousness they can never be united. Freud halted the process at the reduction to the inferior half of the personality and tended to overlook the daemonic dangerousness of the dark side, which by no means consists only of relatively harmless infantilisms. Man is neither so reasonable nor so good that he can cope *eo ipso* with evil. The darkness can quite well engulf him, especially when he finds himself with those of like mind. Mass-mindedness increases unconsciousness and then the evil swells like an avalanche, as contemporary events have shown. Even so, society can also work for good; it is even necessary because of the moral weakness of most human beings, who, to maintain themselves at all, must have some external good to cling on to. The great religions are psychotherapeutic systems that give a foothold to all those who cannot stand by themselves, and they are in the overwhelming majority.

In spite of their undoubtedly "heretical methods" the alchemists showed by their positive attitude to the Church that they were cleverer than certain modern apostles of enlightenment. Also—very much in contrast to the rationalistic tendencies of today—they displayed, despite its "tortuousness," a remarkable understanding of the imagery upon which the Christian cosmos is built. This world of images, in its historical form, is irretrievably lost to modern man; its loss has spiritually impoverished the masses and compelled them to find pitiful substitutes, as poisonous as they are worthless. No one can be held responsible for this development. It is due rather to the restless tempo of spiritual growth and change, whose motive forces go far beyond the horizon of the individual. He can

---

substance...in the beginning whereof is wretchedness with vinegar, but in its ending joy with gladness. And so I supposed it would fare with me, that at first I should taste, endure, and experience many hard, bitter, sad and wearisome things, but at length would see that everything became pleasanter and easier."

only hope to keep pace with it and try to understand it so far that he is not blindly swallowed up by it. For that is the alarming thing about mass movements, even if they are good, that they demand and must demand blind faith. The Church can never explain the truth of her images because she acknowledges no point of view but her own. She moves solely within the framework of her images, and her arguments must always beg the question. The flock of harmless sheep was ever the symbolic prototype of the credulous crowd, though the Church is quick to recognize the wolves in sheep's clothing who lead the faith of the multitude astray in order to destroy them. The tragedy is that the blind trust which leads to perdition is practiced just as much inside the Church and is praised as the highest virtue. Yet our Lord says: "Be ye therefore wise as Serpents,"[180] and the Bible itself stresses the cleverness and cunning of the serpent. But where are these necessary if not altogether praiseworthy qualities developed and given their due? The serpent has become a by-word for everything morally abhorrent, and yet anyone who is not as smart as a snake is liable to land himself in trouble through blind faith.

The alchemists knew about the snake and the "cold" half of nature,[181] and they said enough to make it clear to their successors that they endeavored by their art to lead that serpentine Nous of the darkness, the *serpens mercurialis,* through the stages of transformation to the goal of perfection (*telesmus*).[182] The more or less symbolical or projected integration of the unconscious that went hand in hand with this evidently had so many favorable effects that the alchemists felt encouraged to express a tempered optimism.

---

180. Matthew 10: 16.

181. Hippolytus reports the following saying of the Peratics: "The universal serpent...is the wise word of Eve [σοφὸ τῆς Εὔας λόγος]." This was the mystery and the river of Paradise, and the sign that protected Cain so that no one should kill him, for the God of this world had not accepted his offering. This God reminds us very much of the "prince of this world" in St. John. Among the Peratic it was naturally the demiurge, the "father below." See Legge, *Philosophumena,* 155f.

182. "This is the father of all perfection [*Pater omnis telesmi est hic*]," Julius Ruska, *Tabula Smaragdina: Ein Beitrag zur Geschichte der hermetischen Literatur* (Heidelberg: Carl Winter, 1926), 2.

JAMES HILLMAN

The Suffering of Salt

> *Some seek not gold, but there lives not*
> *a man who does not need salt.*
> —Cassiodorus

Toward a Substantial Psychology

Alchemical salt, like any other alchemical substance, is a meta-phoric or "philosophic" salt. We are warned in various alchemi-cal texts not to assume that this mineral is "common" salt, our table salt or sodium chloride. Yet, as we shall see, this alchemical salt is indeed common to us all—and not only as the physiological content nec-essary to our blood and fluids.[1] It may well be that the epithet "common," which is curiously attached only to salt of all our everyday comestibles,

---

1. Animal life depends on common salt. Horses (according to breed, size and location) require up to 40 pounds a year, cows up to 80. Humans consume about ten pounds (not including the amounts in already prepared edibles). "You and I each con-tain about eight ounces of salt—enough to fill several shakers. [Salt] is involved in mus-cle contractions including heartbeats…nerve impulses…digestion. Without salt the body goes into convulsions, paralysis, death. Put blood cells in a salt-free fluid and they burst." (Gordon Young, "Salt: The Essence of Life," *National Geographic* [September 1977]: 381.) Since the need for salt is so basic, governments relied on salt monopolies and salt taxes for a sure source of funds. Salt-tax rebellions ensued, for salt represented the common people's common need so that its control was an injustice affecting life itself. The defeat of the secessionist South in 1865 has been attributed to a salt famine and a Chinese law states that a man deprived of salt for a fortnight would be too weak to tie up a chicken. (Robert P. Multhauf, *Neptune's Gift: A History of Common Salt* [Bal-timore: The Johns Hopkins University Press, 1978], 3–19.) So valuable was salt that it was imported great distances (for instance, from Sicily via Venice to the peasants in the upper Rhone valleys in Switzerland). In Africa, blocks of Sahara salt were sold to sub-Saharan economies in exchange for gold dust, ivory, and slaves. Salted food is synonymous with "holy" food in ancient Hebrew. (Fernand Braudel, *Civilization and Capitalism, 15th–18th Century,* vol. 1: *The Structures of Everyday Life,* translated by Siân Reynolds [Berkeley: University of California Press, 1992], 209.)

reveals that salt is the substrate of what is meant by "commonly human," so that salt is the archetypal principle of both the sense of the common and common sense. Already you can see how we shall be working in this chapter: we shall be activating the image of salt (1) as a psychological substance, which appears in alchemy as the word *sal*; (2) as an operation, which yields a residue; (3) as any of many physical substances generically called "salts"; and (4) as a property of other substances.

The word *sal* in alchemical texts, especially since Paracelsus, often indicates the stable basis of life, its earth, ground, body. However, the term also more particularly refers to alums, alkalis, crystallizations, bases, ashes, sal ammoniac, potash, as well as to the sense qualities equivalent to these materials: bitterness, astringency, pungency, mordancy, desiccation, and crustiness, dry stings and smarts, sharpness and pointedness.

These qualities of human life belong to the very substance of character. Indeed, bitter and mordant qualities are not only as common and basic as salt, but they are as essential to the embodiment of our psychic nature as is salt in our physical bodies. Our stinging, astringent, dried-out moments are not contingent and accidental; they are of our substance and essence.

This *psychological* approach to salt has two major predecessors: Ernest Jones's "The Symbolic Significance of Salt in Folklore and Superstition" (*Imago* 1 [1912])[2] and C. G. Jung's richly condensed chapter in *Mysterium Coniunctionis* (*CW* 14: 234–348).[3] The main differences between their approaches and mine lie in our different aims. Where they examine salt in a scholarly manner in order to gain an objective meaning of this alchemical substance, I am attempting to bring over to the reader its substantiality as a commonly recognizable experience. Where Jung does a metapsychology of alchemy, I am trying to do an alchemical psychologizing. Hence his chapter on salt, and Jones's mainly anthropological amplification, are indispensable backgrounds, even though they offer less experiential closeness to the material. I intend that my speaking about salt will bear traces of salt with it.

---

2. Reprinted in Ernest Jones, *Essays in Applied Psychoanalysis*, vol. 2: *Essays in Folklore, Anthropology and Religion* (London: Hogarth Press, 1951).

3. Both essays were re-issued and excellently introduced by Stanton Marlan in *Salt and the Alchemical Soul* (Woodstock, Conn.: Spring Publications, 1995).

Our model is the microcosm/macrocosm and the doctrine of correspondences between them. A man or a woman is a smaller arrangement (*kosmos*) which all things in nature are proportionately represented. Not only is the macrocosmic world personified and alive with subjective qualities that we nowadays allow only to human beings, but the microcosm of the human being, because it is a microcosm of nature, is also a mineral, physical object, consisting of substances such as salt. The difference between this psychological substantiality and that of chemistry, which too holds that mineral and physical elements enter into the composition of a human being, is that the chemical model does not require consciousness or soul. There is a radical split between conscious subject and the physical substances. Whereas the alchemical model suggests: as within, so without. The physical world has its interiority and subjectivity because it is a larger arrangement of the soul's nature. For alchemy, both human and world are ensouled. Intelligence, meaning, display—these are potentially present and afforded throughout.

The microcosm/macrocosm model requires a micro/macro-awareness. It asks that we feel into the world of matter with sensitivity for qualitative differences. It asks that we find in our objective experiences analogies with and metaphors of physical processes and substances. The micro/macro model works in two directions. While endowing the world with soul, it also indicates that human nature goes through natural processes of an objectively mineral and metallic sort. Our inner life is part of the natural world order, and this perspective saves us from taking ourselves so personally and identifying what goes on in the soul with the subjective ego. Thus, salts belong to the very stuff of the psyche. *Sal* describes one of our matters, something that is mattering in us and is the "matter" with us—too much, too little salt, or salt at the wrong times and places, or combined wrongly.

Alchemical psychology describes a myriad of substances. William Johnson's *Lexicon Chymicum* of 1652 and Martin Ruland's *Lexicon Alchemiae* of 1612 list hundreds of words referring to materials. These can be reduced to a system of seven basic stuffs deriving from metallic seeds of the traditional planetary gods: all sorts of words may refer to silver, for instance, and its operations, and each of these words connote as well the planetary principle of the moon in a particular phase or guise or combination. A variety of the sevenfold system is that of three substances plus a fourth, the "tetrasoma," which in itself combines four of the primary planetary metals (lead, copper, iron, and tin or antimony). The threefold system, in which salt finds a major place, derives mainly from Paracelsus,[4] the Swiss radical philosopher of nature, religious physician, and eccentric whose system of sulfur, mercury, and salt was a more subtle and chemical mode of imagining than the more gross and metallurgical model of the seven.

Because of the interrelated complexities of these substances, alchemical models are polytheistic, that is, one cannot speak truly of any element alone. Whatever is said about salt is always contaminated, and must be so contaminated by the materials, vessels, and operations with which it is in interaction. Psychic materials are always in diffuse interpenetration, with other materials and do not remain singly self-consistent, and so require multiple interpretation. In fact, this very contamination is part

---

4. Although various of salts were alchemically known in antiquity (Theophrastus, Pliny, and later Geber and Rasis), not until Paracelsus was salt elevated to one of the *tria prima,* more fundamental than the seven planets and the four elemental temperaments. Paracelsus re-founded alchemy on a tripartite scheme by introducing salt as a new third term. This "third" position is characteristic of Paracelsus in that he opposed both Aristotle and the Scholastics on one side and Galen on the other. His tradition, as Walter Pagel shows ("Paracelsus: Traditionalism and Medieval Sources," in *Medicine, Science, and Culture: Historical Essays in Honor of Owsei Temkin,* edited by Lloyd G. Stevenson and Robert P. Multhauf [Baltimore: The Johns Hopkins University Press, 1968], 57 ff.), was Platonic and Neoplatonic, especially in following the tripartite cosmo-anthropology of Marsilio Ficino—body, soul, spirit—whom Paracelsus admired. It is in his advocacy of the third principle that I see the importance of Paracelsus for Jung as a spiritual ancestor (*CW* 15: 1–143; *MDR* 200 and 220). Both warned against theological spiritualism on one side and empirical materialism on the other in order to hold the middle ground of soul or psychic reality. Part of the so-called "elusiveness" of Paracelsus (Owsei Temkin, "The Elusiveness of Paracelsus," *Bulletin of the History of Medicine* 26, no. 3 [May–June 1952]: 201–17) can be attributed to this mercurial middle ground. Although Paracelsus usually identified sulfur rather than salt with the middle integument, it was his advocacy of salt and his own saltiness (the physical, practical, common, vernacular, purgative, sharp-tongued, bitter, uncombinable nature of his character) that shows this substance to have been as fundamental to his nature as it was to his thought. He died, by the way, in Salzburg. (On the three lines of thinking, see Owsei Temkin, *Galenism: Rise and Decline of a Medical Philosophy* [Ithaca: Cornell University Press, 1973], esp. 128–70.)

of their definition: let us say that alchemy is soft-edged. Lines between its elements cannot be drawn hard and fast because these elements are also elementary living natures. The technique of isolation, so essential to the method of modern natural science, arbitrarily forces nature to comply with an isolating kind of consciousness and its epistemology, which cuts, separates, and opposes in order to know.[5]

Alchemical salt is usually in a tandem with sulfur and what is said about salt is usually from a sulfuric standpoint. For example in Paracelsian alchemy, salt is frequently imagined as soul (sulfur as body and mercury as the spirit combining them). The illustrative image is the egg, whose yolk (sulfur)—oily, smelly, sticky and vital—is its body, whose shell (salt)—fixed, inflammable, crusty and enclosing—is its soul, and whose white (mercury)—connecting yolk and shell, mutable, slippery, volatile, changing its shape and consistency—is the egg's spirit. Or the shell (salt) may be the body; the yolk (sulfur), the soul.

I have found that it is better to consider each component to have its own sort of body rather than to insist that salt is always soul (or always body)[6] in a one-to-one equation. We must remember that a psychic substance does not and cannot mean one thing. We find that alchemists shifted "body" to equal this or that depending on the task at hand. The same is true in our psychic work today: certain problems take on body or cry for release from body, or lose their embodiment, so that no single aspect of our psychic lives can consistently be named "body." As Robert Sardello has often said, body is most elusive. When body is equated with sulfur what is meant is the excitable, palpable urgency, the body of generative passions and will. When body is called salt what is meant is the fixed, consistent, stable body that encloses any existent as its outer shell. Paradoxically, salt may mean the inner core: for salt was imagined by Khunrath as the center of the earth. Perhaps the best way to understand "body" in this context is by the action of a substance: that which coagulates or brings embodiment about therefore must itself be body.

---

5. "Science" from *scire*, to know, is cognate with *scindere*, to cut, divide, and has the same probable root as schism, shed, and shit (as separation). Cf. Ernest Weekley, *An Etymological Dictionary of Modern English* (London: John Murray, 1921.)

6. Cf. *CW* 14: 322–23. Salt is also Christ, Mercurius, and thus the spirit as well as the soul, and body or earth.

Sometimes sulfur is the coagulatory agent; sometimes coagulation is attributed to the power of salt.

The tandem of salt and sulfur continues in modern lives and modern dreams. A woman in analysis oscillates between burning enthusiasms for new people, projects, places. She is ready to catch fire at any moment, bringing a richly fat imagination and vital energy to life. She also has times of depression: drinking alone self-enclosed, encrusted, bitter with residues of what has been, stuck for hours in a square chair at a square table, feeling low and base, sunk to the center of the earth. There is no direct connection between her sulfur and her salt. They oscillate in "mood swings." An alchemical therapeutic approach would not temper one with the other, but would touch both with mercury, that is, free them from their alternating concretism by means of psychological insight. The first step is to see how impersonally autonomous the swings are and how they constellate each other, as do sulfur and salt.

In another case, a young man, finding it hard to yield some of his childish innocence and the rich life in the lap of the mother and the gods, dreams first of walking with his girl through a salt desert, then of their sharing salty meat together, and then of a strange man who runs a stand on the street, handing the dreamer a salty sausage-type roll instead of what he had ordered—a roll or bun filled with yellow, sweet-cream custard. The dreamer is offended. He had wanted the savor and joy of sulfur in the sweet soft things that slip down with no effort.[7] But the strange man-in-the-street (Mercurius himself, perhaps) hands him the bitter sting of salt that can bring tears to one's eyes. We shall now have to explore the nature of this salt.

Salt Mines: The Mining and Making of Salt

But first—where is the salt to be found? How do we mine it, make it, prepare it. Eirenaeus Philalethes replies: "...descend into yourself, for you carry it about with you." It is to be found in "Man's blood out of the body, or man's urine."[8] Mark well that those bodies which flow forth from our

---

7. A classical psychoanalyst would likely find the contrast between sausage roll and creamy bun to symbolize an opposition between male and female genitalia.

8. "The Secret of the Immortal Liquor called ALKAHEST or IGNIS-AQUA," in

bodies are salts and alums."[9] As there is salt in the macrocosm, so can it be mined from within microcosmic human nature. In fact, because salt is "the natural balsam of the living body" (*Paracelsus,* 1: 259) we descend into the experiential component of this body—its blood, sweat, tears, and urine—to find our salt. Jung (*CW*14: 330) considers alchemical salt to refer to feelings and to Eros; I would specify his notion further by saying that salt is the mineral, impersonal, objective ground of personal experience making experience possible. No salt, no experiencing—merely a running on and running through of events without psychic body.[10]

Thus salt makes events sensed and felt, giving us each a sense of the personal—my tears, my sweat and blood, my taste and value. The entire alchemical opus hangs on the ability to experience subjectively. Hence it is said in *The Golden Tract*: "He who works without salt will never raise dead bodies."[11] The matters are only macrocosmic and chemical, out there, dead, unless one works with salt. These intensely personal experiences are nonetheless common to all—both intensely mine and yet common as blood, as urine, as salt. In other words, salt acts like the ground of subjectivity ("That which is left at the bottom of our distilling vessel is our salt—that is to say our earth."[12]). It makes possible what psychology calls felt experience. We must turn to this same ground to mine our salt.

"Felt experience" takes on a radically altered meaning in the light of alchemical salt. We may imagine our deep hurts not merely as wounds to be healed but as salt mines from which we gain a precious essence and without which the soul cannot live. The fact that we return to these deep hurts, in remorse and regret, in resentment and revenge, indicates a psychic need beyond a mere mechanical repetition compulsion. Instead, the soul has a drive to remember; it is like an animal that returns to its salt licks; the soul licks at its own wounds to derive sustenance therefrom. We

Eirenaeus Philalethes, *Collectanea Chymica: A Collection of Ten Several Treatises in Chemistry Concerning the Liquor Alkahest, the Mercury of Philosophers, and other Curiosities Worthy the Perusal* (London: William Cooper, 1684), 6 and 8.

9. *The Golden Tract Concerning the Stone of the Philosophers* (*HM* 1: 22).

10. In common cookery salt is used for "contracting" the fibers of meat. *Mrs. Beeton's Household Management* (Ware, Hertfordshire: Wordsworth Editions, 2006), 269.

11. *The Golden Tract* (*HM* 1: 22).

12. Ibid.

make salt in our suffering and, by keeping faith with our sufferings, we gain salt, healing the soul of its salt-deficiency. D. H. Lawrence said:

> I am not a mechanism, an assembly of various sections. And it is not because the mechanism is working wrongly, that I am ill. I am ill because of wounds to the soul, to the deep emotional self and the wounds to the soul take a long, long time, only time can help and patience, and a certain difficult repentance. [13]

The alchemical substances offer distinctions in kinds of suffering. Salt, for instance, may be distinguished from lead, in that the first is sharp, stinging, acute: it burns in on itself with wit and bite, corrosive acrimony, making sense through self-accusation and self-purification. It is purgative. Lead, however, is chronic and dense, a heavy, oppressive, gloomy suffering, without specified focus, senseless. It is constipative. Whereas salt says "it hurts," lead says "I can't." Where salt tastes the details of its pain by remembering precisely and with piercing agony, lead cannot see, does not know, remaining paralyzed and sunk in a general, abstract obliteration of empirical memory.

The curing of these conditions also differs: salt requires a pinch, feeling the pinch of the event that stings; lead seems to require time, waiting it through, that patience Lawrence speaks of. What results from the salt cure is a new sense of what happened, a new appreciation of its virtue for soul. The result of the lead cure is depth, weight and gravity, more fullness and the ability to "hold it" and "bear it." The two contrast also in two literary genres of suffering: irony (salt) and tragedy (lead). The first tends toward common human experience while the second tends to give distance from that experience. Of course, there are "leaden salts" in alchemy, that is, conditions in which the leaden and the salty aspects of suffering are so combined that the distinctions are hard to notice: usually that which dulls and blankets the nature of salt is a result of lead. The task becomes one of separating lead from salt, black mood from recollection, poisoned spirit from subjective experience, the fateful inescapable destiny from the personally culpable wrong-doing.

---

13. "Healing," in *The Complete Poems of D. H. Lawrence* (Ware, Hertfordshire: Wordsworth Editions, 1994), 513.

Salt may also be mined from whatever is stable. As the principle of stability whose alchemical sign was a square,[14] salt can be mined from the rocks of concrete experience, those fixities which mark our lives with defined positions. These places are not merely solid facts—my degree, my property, my car accident, my abortion, my war record, my divorce; these are also places where psychic body is salted away and stored. These rocks, when recognized and owned, belong to the history of my soul, where it has been salted down by the fixities of experience, giving a certain crystallization to my nature and keeping me from inflammations and volatilizations.

As salt is not flammable,[15] it seems not subject to heat: we make salt less in ardor than in recrimination, less by desire than by memory of desire. "Ash on an old man's sleeve / Is all the ash the burnt roses leave" (T. S. Eliot, "Little Gidding"). Ash is the memory of the fire; not a burnt-out cinder, but the fixed inflammable essence of a love that once flamed to heaven.

Though we cannot make it by fire, we do make salt by means of dissolutions. Salt is soluble. Weeping, bleeding, sweating, urinating bring salt out of its interior underground mines. It appears in our moistures, which are the flow of salt to the surface. "During the work the salt assumes the appearance of blood" (*CW*14: 337). Moments of dissolution are not mere collapses; they release a sense of personal human value from the encrustations of habit. "I, too, am a human being worth my salt"—hence my blood, sweat, and tears.

---

14. See Herbert Silberer, *Problems of Mysticism and its Symbolism*, translated by Smith Ely Jelliffe (New York: Moffat, Yard and Company, 1917), 395–96. Concerning salt as square or cube, Silberer makes a nice differentiation: "Crystallization produces the regular form; fixation, the density." The scanning electron microscope shows the structure of common salt to be rather like hard-edged squares or small flat cubes. Cf. the alchemist Edward Jorden (1569–1632) in Allen G. Debus, *English Paracelsians* (London: Oldbourne Press, 1965), 163.

15. On fire and salt, see Jung, *CW*14: 319. The "fire" hidden in salt is its dry power or spirit even if it remains itself inflammable. Common sodium chloride melts only at 800° C. Yet there is a "fire" hidden in salt, for common table salt is composed of "a metal so unstable that it bursts into flame when exposed to water; and a lethal gas (chlorine)" (Young, "Salt," 381).

It is curious how we are fixated upon our wounds. Psychology speaks of trauma, invented a traumatic theory of neurosis and post-traumatic stress disorder. Why does psychology go back to the hurt child for grounding psychic development, and why does the psyche itself need to look back? It seems the soul must have its signal remembrance engraved into its psychic body so that it knows it has or is a body. Pain implicates us at once in body, and psychic pain in psychic body. We are always *subjected* to pain, so that events that hurt, like childhood traumas, abuse, and rape, force our subjectivity upon us. These events seem in memory to be more real than any others because they carry the force of subjective reality.

Viewed from the perspective of salt, early traumas are moments of initiation into the sense of being a "me" with a subjective personal interior. We tend to fixate on *what* was done to us and *who* did it: resentment, revenge. But what psychologically matters is *that* it was done: the blow, the blood, the betrayal. Like the ashes which are rubbed into the wounds at initiation rites to purify and scarify, the soul is marked by its trauma. Salt still is touched to the body in Christian Baptism, and eaten still at Jewish Pessach in ritual remembrance of trauma.[16] A trauma is a salt mine; it is a fixed place for reflection about the nature and value of my personal being, where memory originates and looking back into personal history begins. These traumatic events initiate in the soul a sense of its embodiment as a vulnerable experiencing subject.

The paradigmatic story of "looking back" is that of Lot's wife (Genesis 19: 26). (Lot and Lot's wife were even used as alchemical terms for salt—cf. Johnson's *Dictionary.*) Because Lot's wife could not refrain from looking back at the destruction of Sodom from which they had been saved, she was turned to a pillar of salt. Jewish commentators[17] say

---

16. The touch of salt and bitter herbs at Jewish Passover brings back the memorial image of the Red Sea and the desert. The image must not be forgotten because it is part of what makes this day different from any other day, i.e., remembrances help differentiate and fix significance. Salt initiates the youngest child (naive soul) into the bitter images of the soul. When, however, remembrance becomes more than a touch, over-salted, then "not forgetting" becomes literalized into history as facts. Then we become stuck in the past rather than sticking to the image, and the salt acts no longer as an imagistic remembrance, but becomes a literalized historical experience.

17. Louis Ginzberg, *The Legends of the Jews,* 7 vols. (Baltimore: The Johns Hopkins

that her mother-love made her look behind to see whether her married daughters were following; and Christian comments on Luke 17: 32 (Clement of Alexandria, *Exhortation to the Greeks,* 94) also see the source of her move in remembrances of family and relatives, personal subjectivities of feeling. Evidently, family fixations are also salt-mines. The disappointments, worries, smarts of mother-complex love—the evening with the photograph album, the keepsakes—are ways the psyche produces salt, returning to events in order to turn them into experiences.

The danger here is always fixation, whether in recollection, earlier trauma, or in a literalized and personalized notion of experience itself: "I am what I have experienced." Paracelsus defined salt as the principle of fixation (*Paracelus* 2: 366).[18] This term, like projection, condensation, sublimation, reappears centuries later in psychoanalysis where it is defined by Freud:

> Fixation can be described in this way. One instinct or instinctual component fails to accompany the rest along the anticipated normal path of development, and, in consequence...it is left behind at a more infantile stage.[19]

Here we have Genesis 19: 26 recapitulated in modern psychoanalytic language. The image of Lot's family on its journey is now presented as a "path of development." Parable becomes theory; the story salted down as science.

Among these sources of salt, urine holds a special place.[20] According to the model of the macrocosm/microcosm, urine is the human brine. It is the microscopic sea within, or the "waters below." Jewish legends[21]

University Press, 1998), 1: 255 and 5: 241–42. The same commentaries note that the destructive rain that fell on Sodom while Lot's wife was looking back on that place of lustful desire was a rain of brimstone (sulfur), i.e., salt longing for sulfur.

18. Cf. John Read, *Prelude to Chemistry: An Outline of Alchemy, Its Literature and Relationships* (London: G. Bell and Sons, 1936), 27.

19. "Psycho-Analytic Notes Upon an Autobiographical Account of a Case of Paranoia," in Sigmund Freud, *Collected Papers,* 4 vols. (London: Hogarth Press, 1924–25), 3: 453.

20. Cf. Philalethes, "The Secret of the Immortal Liquor called ALKAHEST" for a short treatise on urine. For a recipe of "piss and vinegar," see *The Testament of Cremer* (*HM* 2: 74). The urine is to be collected from an "unpolluted [virginal] youth."

21. Ginzberg, *Legends of the Jews,* 5: 18.

explain that salt is included in all sacrifices as a remembrance of the act of Creation by the separation of the waters above from those below, their having been torn asunder, and the salt remembers these lower waters and their weeping at having been cast down from nearness with God.

Urinary salts are residual traces afloat in the lower person. They are essential remembrances that betray our inner nature, its color, smell, opacity. Bladder disorders and urinary symptoms and dreams may refer to an awakening to the lower waters, to the fact that there is psychic life in the lower person independent of what goes on above, and this life is all intense, burning, personal necessity, which no one else can tend for you and for which time and place and privacy must be found.

A patient dreams: "My urine is to be examined with various chemicals. I have in front of me several glass bottles with different chemicals, but I don't know how much to take of each of the chemicals for each of the little bottles and how I am to get my urine into these little bottles."

Psychoanalysis as urinalysis suggests very careful discriminations of private, internal residues, and making clear (glass) distinctions among them. It is as if the urinary salts must be separated from generalized memory and generalized suffering and examined for their quite specific particulars. For the dreamer the task is double: *dosage* (how much to take) and *focus* (capturing the flow in narrowly accurate perceptions). It is an exercise in "eachness"—a term fondly used by William James to counter the global thinking and feeling of wholeness.

Urine of the virgin boy (between eight and twelve years) was often mentioned as a starting substance for the work. This "urine of the boy" is one of the many names for the *materia prima*. It refers to the salts in the microcosmic sea before the Fall, that is, the archetypal essence of each particular character before it has accumulated personal residues: salt not as the result of events, but as prior to events. The virginal condition is not empty or blank, even if unsullied by experience. These salts have their own specific gravity and qualities—that is, there is an *a priori* salt in our "boy of the soul," who is defined by the fixed intensities that are the demanding urgencies of ones own particular essence. The salts in the urine of the boy are these archetypal traces of character essence. Platonic remembrances that are virginal because they are given intact with one's nature and that can be opened by the alchemical opus.

Johnson's *Dictionary* states simply: *"Urina puerorum est mercurius."* Of course, Mercurius's names are legion; when, however, a substance is overtly named such, there is immediate significance for soul-making. This implies that the ambitions of puer fantasy, which Freudian psychology has attributed to the urinary phase of the little boy's development, take on revelatory significance. It is not merely "urinary erotism"[22]—that I can sexually fertilize the world or extinguish its fires or start rivulets. The urinary ambition of the "boy of the soul" is also an expression of my salt, the essence of myself, my base. "Look," it says, "see my piss—this is me." There is a potent spirit to be found in the silly piss of one's little boy (even perhaps in his bed-wetting).

We can feel the primordial salt of the puer in the bitter pains of ambition that burn before any accomplishment, and also in the sense of remorse that stings before there have been external events to rue. Burning intensities can plague a childhood before worldly experience has begun, and these same salty pains reappear when the boy of the soul is constellated. In the *urina puerorum* is a remembrance of things *a priori* that load an act in the world with more salt than puer consciousness can sometimes bare: huge guilts, high-pitched hopes, even suicide. For the puer comes not only on wings of flights and in games of love; he comes, too, smarting with a memory of beauty and what one is on earth for.

The *urina puerorum* suggests that with the right operation we can recover the salty aspect of the puer. The salt to put on the tail of puer flights is already there to begin with, if we but know the right operation for recovering it. One operation which alchemy suggests for making salt is evaporation.

The watery boy who floats in and out with the tides of emotion and follows the streams of least resistance can be fixed by the salts buried in his own tissues. These give regularities, densities, squareness, and body. When the tides of the sea are exposed to sunlight and their flow stopped, salt crystallizes; so can salt be gained by the evaporation of the microcosmic flood. For this operation, alchemists used a wide-open, flat pan; all things exposed in broad daylight and all the upward pressure allowed

---

22. Henry A. Murray, "American Icarus," in *Puer Papers,* edited by James Hillman (Irving, Texas: Spring Publications, 1979), 91 ff.

to escape. The steam, the smoke, and the cloudy vapors ascend to dissipate in hot air. We lose the lushness of feelings, the flush of high hopes, the dumb bogs of inertia; and, as the moistures recede, something essential crystallizes in the dry air. Here, the sealed hermetic vessel would be wrong. Evaporation means not taking events deeply and intensively but rather flattening the affects and letting a pressure steam away by itself until it comes down to itself. Evaporation to a salt: this is the common salt of the everyday table of the world which is at the same time one's own crystallized experience of it.[23]

The alchemical idea that urine contained a potent spirit, a mercurial *lumen naturalis* (light of nature) became evident in 1669 when the German Hennig Brand—called the "last of the alchemists"—cooked urine mixed with sand and produced a soapy residue that glowed.[24] Phosphorous had been discovered. The word etymologically means "light-bringing." It is an epithet for the morning star, for Lucifer, and for Hermes. Indeed, *urina puerorum est mercurius.*

The When and How of Salting

Albertus Magnus declares: "Salt is necessary for every solution."[25] This seems a strange statement, inasmuch as we have been imagining salt as the principle of fixity, of bitter crustiness. Solutions, in contrast, seem to connote fluid, passive, receptive conditions, allowing bitterness to dissolve and crustiness to melt. The *solutio*, however, in alchemical psychology is one of the very few basic operations and because of its ubiquity throughout the entire opus, it cannot be defined in only one way. Evidently, a genuine solution must have the capacity to stabilize. It must sustain a condition, not merely dissolve it.

The alchemical *solutio* does not suggest simplified problem-solving. Rather, it requires salt in order to affect the material in a lasting

---

23. Since there are many salts, there are many operations to produce it, evaporation being but one. Others are calcination, putrefaction, distillation (salt as a by-product), coagulation.

24. Isaac Asimov, *The Search for the Elements* (New York: Basic Books, 1962), 35–36; cf. Robert P. Multhauf, *The Origins of Chemistry* (London: Oldbourne, 1966), 22f.

25. Albertus Magnus, *Libellus de alchimia,* translated by Virginia Heines (Berkeley: University of California Press, 1958), 61.

way. The salt mines of which we spoke in the previous section are both deposits of salt and attempts at solution. When we sit still and sweat it out, we are stabilizing and adding salt to the solution so that it becomes a genuine one. Problems seem not to go away until they have first been thoroughly received.

The issue at stake here is the capacity to internalize, to admit and receive a problem into one's inner nature as one's inner nature. This would be to salt it. A problem reaches its solution only when it is adequately salted, for then it touches us personally, penetrating to that point where we can say: *"Fiat mihi*; all right; I admit, I give in; it's really my problem; it has to be." The taste of this experience is bitter, and it humiliates, and it lasts—a lasting solution.

A second use for salt is in order to "slay sulfur."[26] Remember: salt is square and blue,[27] and it coagulates. When sulfur flares up it can be slain by a pinch of salt, the pinch that kills, whether a tearful eye, a sharp-tongued remark, a grain of common sense. Salt wounds and slays the impulsive reactions, because it recalls the pain incurred in similar events. Salt gives us the awareness of repetition; sulfur, only the compulsion. Perhaps the exalted *sal sapientia* (salt of wisdom, wisdom of salt) is nothing more grandiose than salt's ability to inhibit sulfur.

As there are psychologies of sulfur that preach action and base themselves on desire, drive, and will, examining psychological events in terms of behavior and its reinforcement or control, so there are psychologies of salt. These tend to literalize the idea that personal suffering is necessary for every solution. They insist upon the self-improvement of interior life. They advocate guilt and penance and working through, examining subjective history, personal feelings, traumata. Alchemical psychology corrects this sort of literalizing by presenting the personal factor that so dominates in psychologies of salt to be impersonal and commonly general. Then, when we work at our self-correction, betterment, purification, we realize that it is not the self that is the focus of our good work;

---

26. *The New Chemical Light* (*HM* 1: 154–55).

27. Debus, *The English Paracelsians*, 163: "Salts are proper to blew colors" (citing Edward Jorden's *A Discourse of Naturall Bathes, and Minerall Waters* [London: Thomas Haprer, 1631]). Jorden also wrote probably the first treatise in English on hysteria.

it is the salt. We are simply working on the salt. In this way, the salt in alchemical psychology helps keep the work from flaming up in the ego-istic inflation of personal guilt. I am alone responsible; it's all my fault.

Salt is especially missing in young people. A young and careless man dreams of visiting Jung in his house, which turns out to be a laboratory in a huge salt dome where a wizened Jung explains how he works on mak-ing salt. Another young man full of promise and void of accomplishment dreams of a beautiful, running deer that springs into a river, its antlers high above the water, crosses, and then collapses on the other bank in desper-ate need of salt. A transition of the spirit had been made, but only through exhaustion does it come home to the dreamer how badly he needs to con-serve, not only his leaping, bounding, rutting spirit but also the experi-ences of his dream life where his spirit shows itself. Unless the animals of his imagination are salted they may simply vanish in spiritual heroics and aesthetic highs. Yes, we catch the bird by putting salt on its tail.

Why is young love so bitter and study for exams so bloody? Are these not rituals of the salt, ways of intensifying that thicken matters and cement them in place? Bitter love is a salt cure, curing the tender soul, with tears, recriminations and, finally, some sort of stabilized pattern. The backwards and forwards of lovers' fights between tearing passion and passionate tears enact stages of the salt/sulfur conjunction. The salt component "that just won't let go" helps preserve the relationship, when sulfur would burn it out or turn it black.

As macrocosmic salt keeps meat and fish, and pickles vegetables, so we need salt in microcosmic ecology for fixing, toughening, preserving. We can't swallow and digest all that happens in a day, or in a night—so we need long hours of pickling events in glass jars for later staring at, shar-ing and consuming. If we would keep something, we salt it down, salt it away. The decaying impulse of young nature—the fresher and purer the substance, the surer and sooner it rots—is held in abeyance. Salt gives us time, endurance, survival. It seasons youth by removing excess mois-ture, thereby preserving the soul through dryness. Dry souls are best, said Heraclitus, which Philo turned to mean, "Where the earth is dry, the soul is wisest"—*sal sapientia*. Analysis shrinks.

"Salt causes matters to thicken." It acts as "knot and cement."[28] What modern psychology speaks of as "integration of personality" and "integrity of character," alchemical psychology refers to as salt, for it is this sophic substance that effects internal adhesion, knitting and knotting events into experience, shrinking generalities into specifics. Salt gives the sense of significant detail, crystallizations that pack with importance what might otherwise have been a bland evening of "waste sad time stretching before and after" (T. S. Eliot, "Burnt Norton"). We want to meet someone at the party who can put sting into a conversation. At a family affair it is usually a crusty old Aunt or Grandfather who adds the salt. The flow of unexperienced events suddenly condenses and remains fixed as we are shriveled by a penetratingly salty observation.

There is another time and place for salt: when the soul needs earthing. When dreams and events do not feel real enough, when the uses of the world taste stale, flat and unprofitable, when we feel uncomfortable in community and have lost our personal "me-ness"—weak, alienated, drifting—then the soul needs salt. We mistake our medicine at times and reach for sulfur: action, false extraversion, trying harder. However, the move toward the macrocosm may first have to go back toward the microcosm, so that the world can be *experienced* and not merely joined with and acted upon as an abstract field. World must become earth; and this move from world as idea to tangible presence requires salt.

Ruland says: "Nothing can be tangible without the presence of salt." Salty language, salty wit, salty sailors, soldier's pay (*salarium* = salary), worth one's salt, a salted bill, a salted bitch (lustful), a dose of salts—these express the tangible values of the base, workaday, and common earth that our feet walk upon and our hands touch. This language of salt connotes each human being as "salt of the earth": only those well-born and high-placed can afford to sit "above the salt."

The mines of common experience offer this salt: the saws and skilled physical know-how of the old-timer, the age-old crystallizations

28. D. R. Oldroyd, "Some Neoplatonic and Stoic Influences on Mineralogy in the Sixteenth and Seventeenth Centuries," *Ambix* 21 (1974): 148 (citing the French alchemist Nicolas Le Fèvre [1615–1669]).

of common law and common speech. Each of these is like a salt mine, and we can bring down our high-falutin' notions and half-cocked ideas by earthing them in commonality. Salt gives what one has in one's head a worth among people, a tangible value on earth. Commonality, however, needs to be distinguished, from being practical and finding application. To earth an image is not simply to sell an invention. Rather, to salt or earth one's winged speculations is to express them with a common touch; tangibility of style.

Earth is also a local sense. There is salt in local speech: accent, patois, dialect, idioms. Whether one-liners that are grainy epitomes (New York) or drawn out tales that meander across the land (Texas), local speech makes words tangible. The difference between dialect and dialectics, between patois and jargon, between earthy humor and dirty joke, between local idiomatic and national idiotic ("televisionese") is all a matter of salt.

"Salt is not added in equal portions to every kind of food; and this circumstance should be diligently considered by the physician" (*Paracelsus* I: 264). Now we are talking about dosage. Salt requires particularizing; it forces one to take note of the specific taste of each event. Tangibility means recognition and discrimination of specific natures. This sheds a new light upon the idea of the common; it is evidently not merely collective and general. What is common, however, is a sense for the particular—the water in this village is softer and sweeter than the water on the other side of the valley; these game birds need to hang another day; you can't use that kind of nail in this kind of wood; when the fever turns into sweating, you have to give even more liquids. Paracelsian medicine turned to the patient and tried to make acute differential perceptions; yet it also tried to be a medicine of and for the common people in earthy dialect. We have perverted the meaning of "common" to denote *all* or *usual* or *equal*; whereas "common salt," alchemically speaking, refers to the sharp perception of inherent natures that brings out their individual properties so that we can understand the right dosage.

As we become salty, the caution of salting tends to reverse. Where once it was necessary to catch the bird and conserve experiences, we begin to find ourselves slowly pickling in brine. Events don't let us go: they return to our heart's blood, leap with tears to the eye, bring us to break out in cold sweat over a past deed, burn in the bladder. (Paracelsus speaks of the "evil there is in salt" [1: 259].) No longer the conscious application of salt, salting now becomes autonomously psychic. The soul forces its tangibility upon us and brings home our common and base susceptibility to human pain. Perhaps this is the eros of salt Jung writes about, or the wisdom of it, or the black earth and shadow associated at times with salt in alchemy; or perhaps it is the ashes and dry earth to which we are returning, the soul's essence becoming fixed, intimations of immortality that first feel like personal pain.

Paracelsus writes (1: 43): "Salt corrects and fixes leprous Luna, cleansing it from its blackness." Thus salt is also a "corrective"—and particularly a corrective of lunatic nigredo conditions by fixing them. A bitter despair, a drawn-out moody meanness, a corrosive worry, a stubborn self-ignorance are leprous. These conditions eat through their own skin, spread contagiously. One picks at oneself. These conditions make the reflective power, which belongs with Luna, splotchy, coming out only in spots, here and there, tatters of whiteness that leprously perpetuate the condition rather than clearing it. Although "leprous" in alchemy generally meant "impure," Paracelsus seems to be speaking of a sickness of reflection itself, when the powers of the moon become sicklied over, Hamlet-style. Rather than having the body of a clear insight, such reflections attack one's own embodiment—my actions, my nature, my self.

Salt corrects this illness of reflection by means of fixing precisely what it is that is wrong. The blackness refers to the generalized stain obscuring reflection, those introspective attempts to see into the dark that only further darken the mind. The acute attack of salt particularizes the mental state by means of a precision of feeling. Exactly what, when, where, and how must be felt, so that the "general mess of imprecision of feeling" (T. S. Eliot, "East Coker") can be spotted, and each spot cleared one by one. The larger disaster is corrected by the smaller sense of it. Accuracy means acuteness; painful to the self-eating wasting disease while cleansing it of too much lunar reflection.

A woman dreams of a small, bottomless lake of salt and there are warnings to stay out of the water. She falls in and the water is so thick that it doesn't feel liquid. A long piece of salt catches her right arm and begins to pull her under. With effort she disengages from it and manages to climb out by finding toeholds in crevices of solidified salt along the bank. Public, collective opinion warns against what it sees as a bottomless salt pit of depression. But she falls in, despite prudent opinion and her intention. When she is in this lake, it is so dense and coagulated that the water no longer flows. Stuck. (Salt causes matter to thicken, says one of our texts.) Here this thickening is like the process of identification: she has become immersed in the thickness of her suffering, which at the same time is the place of her becoming more cohesive, stable and solid. One piece of this generalized lake of salt, one crystallized moment of it—a remembrance, a guilt, a bitter point of pain—catches her arm of action and pulls her further inward and downward. Disengagement happens by effort, particularly by finding toeholds in already memorial, crystallized experience from which the moisture has dried out. She can actually make her way out by standing upon what she has already been through. She is afforded a way out of the bottomless lake by standing on a solid "bank," by "banking" on something solid that is there whenever the bottomless lake is there. The way out is at the edge, her marginalization. Like cures like: the disengagement from identification with salt takes place *not* through the efforts of the right arm which only drag her further under, but through small basic understandings that can be found in the little depressions and faults (crevices) of her solidified subjective experience.

The Fervor of Salt

Our account has attempted to bring home the experience of salt in alchemical psychology. We have come to see salt to be the ground of subjectivity. Salt fixates, corrects, crystallizes and purifies, all of which it can do to subjectivity itself. This purification of subjectivity shall more particularly occupy us in this final section where the connection more clearly emerges between salt and virginity.

We have already met its hard and square, densive-protective nature. For example: the egg analogy of Paracelsus, where salt was the shell; and in the writings of Joseph Duchesne (Quercetanus, c. 1544–1609), where salt appears in the hard matter of things, their roots, bark and bones, those parts that are clotted, cemented, coagulated or congealed.[29]

29. Debus, *The English Paracelsians,* 94 (citing Duchesne's *Le Grand miroir du monde* [Paris, 1595]).

We may go so far as attributing to this substance that tendency in writings about salt to conclude with a clotted thought, a reduction to a basic idea. The multiple nature of salts, their multiple origins and effects, that the term refers to so many different qualities of experience and chemical materials (alums, alkalis, ashes, etc.)[30]—all tend to congeal into a single basic principle. For Jones this idea was "semen"; for Jung, it was "Eros." The stuff of which we write becomes the stuff with which we write and we are affected by the material we work with. As we would take in the reader, captivating and convincing, so does the material because it, too, is ensouled, captures our imagination: we lose mercurial volatility and sulfuric richness and become reduced ourselves to repetitions, moral constraints and fixities of expression as we attempt to go ever inward, accurately defining the pure roots and bones, crystallizing that experience called *"sal."* The importance of salt as value (expressed above in terms of soldier's pay) instead becomes an overvaluation of either the place of this substance within the alchemical opus or of one's interpretation: an overvalued idea due to an overdose of salt.

This effect of salt proceeds from its own fervor, *a fervor of fixity,* which can be distinguished from the fervor of sulfuric enthusiasm and its manic boil of action, as well as from the fervor of mercury and its effervescent volatility. Salt's fervor is rather holy, cleansing and bitter; immovably fixed; fanatic.

You will recall that Paracelsus (1: 258) held that we eat salt to cherish our nature of salt and that we desire salt for its own sake. Salt desires itself. Its appetite works in us and through us for itself. It is fixed upon itself. Where sulfur and mercury are found in and by means of other events, salt is the experience of feeding on experience. By closing out the other principles, it can intensify its own interiority. A salt mine right there in whatever we call "mine." Thus *in extremis,* salt eats into its own nature, corrosive as lye in its own self-reflective purifications: recriminations,

---

30. For a treatise showing many salts and the different operation for each, see Robert Steele, "Practical Chemistry in the Twelfth Century," *Isis* 12 (1929): 10–21. (Rasis's practices are reported in Bonus of Ferrara, *The New Pearl of Great Price: A Treatise Concerning the Treasure and Most Precious Stone of the Philosophers or the Method and Procedure of this Divine Art,* translated by Arthur Edward Waite [London: Vincent Stuart, 1963], 366–71.)

repentance, ashes, lustrations toward an ever-purer essence. Its suffering is self-caused. This is the salt that turns all reds to blue—blue in the senses of cold, puritan, celestial, exclusive, loyal, doleful, deadly (cyanide, cobalt, prussic).[31]

Here we may review those images of pure salt that we have already seen: of the virgin boy's urine, white crystal, final ash. Here, too, belong the images of the salt desert as if it were heaven: the Elysian fields become a Dead Sea, celestial, immaculate and barren, a crystalline ground of self-laceration, that sense of being grounded in long-suffering nobility, which negates even the *fiat mihi*. For nothing comes from the Great Salt Lake when one has oneself become purely salt, like Lot's wife. As salt fixates and purifies itself, suffering becomes fanaticism.

The intensity of this fanaticism appears in alchemical language both as ammonia, caustic soda, alkali, white lime, and as natron, the white salt of niter, which is a destructive, explosive powder. (Even table salt is delicately flammable, an unstable metal—sodium.)

Some alchemists recognized as salts whatever appeared in crystalline form. May we imagine that a salt crystallizes to bind its inherent fervor? These fanatical salts manifest themselves more in political and doctrinal affairs, although similar attitudes appear as well in the concretistic *askesis* of paranoid schizophrenia. The very virtue of salt—its down-to-earth, concrete commonality—seems a virtue only in combination with other elements. Alone, salt fixates on itself, attempting to become the pure elixir which alchemy insists is always the result of many combinations.

The inherent capability of salt to crystallize its own essence is what I would call the inherent virginity of salt. By virginity here I mean the self-same, self-enclosed devotion to purity. I believe it is this aspect of salt that is alchemically associated with the cold, hard aspect of Luna, the queen as "bitch."[32] The Luna-sal connection is discussed at length by Jung, who considers salt another term for the moon, another manifestation of the more general principle of "the feminine."[33]

---

31. Cf. below, Chapter 5: "Alchemical Blue and the *Unio Mentalis.*"

32. *CW* 14: 174 ff. Robert Grinnell (*Alchemy in a Modern Woman* [Dallas: Spring Publications, 1973]), expands upon the "bitch" in depth.

33. *CW* 14: 234, 240, and 320–55.

In ancient Rome, salt was indeed the province of the virginal feminine, the Vestals.34 They prepared the sacrificial animals and sprinkled
each with salt to make it holy. The Vestal (i.e., an initiated and ritualized)
Virgin was the mistress of the salt; she understood how to handle it. Here
is the virgin, not in the fervor of fanaticism, but the virgin as *mediatrix;*
she knows the right dosage, a pinch, a touch, a grain, not a state. Jung
quotes Picinellus: "Let the word be sprinkled with salt, not deluged with
it."35 The dosage of salt is an art: it must be taken *cum grano salis*, not corrosive, bitter irony and biting sarcasm or fixed immortal dogma, but the
deft touch that brings out the flavor. Even the salt of wisdom (*sal sapientia*)
and the salt of common sense become crystallized and destructive when
taken alone, squarely, or imagined straight, for it is in the very nature of
salt to literalize itself and conserve itself into a crystal body. Any insight or
experience preserved as truth or faith becomes virginal: it closes into itself,
becomes unyielding, dense and defended. Too much salt. We are each virginal when we are preserved from experience by preserved experience.

Hence the importance of the Vestal Virgins. Like cures like. Their
conscious virginity enabled them to handle the purifying power of the
salt. As initiates in the cult of salt, they must have understood the dangers
of its "corruptive ferment."36 Society is always in danger of the fervor of
salt—puritanism, fanaticism, terrorism—and the preservation of Roman
culture depended upon the Vestal Virgins.37 This suggests that a psychological understanding of the power of salt and its dosage is necessary for
the human body, the soul's body, and the body politic. Too little and principles go by the board; too much and a reign of terror ensues.

We can recognize when the principle of fixation has become a fixation of principle. Then salt is unable to be combusted and released by
sulfur or is unable to be touched or stained by mercury: neither life nor

---

34. Stephanie A. Demetrakopoulos, "Hestia, Goddess of the Hearth," *Spring: An
Annual of Archetypal Psychology and Jungian Thought* (1979): 65–68, with notes. For
details of the preparation of the *mola*, see Georges Dumézil, *Archaic Roman Religion*,
translated by Philip Krapp, 2 vols. (Baltimore: The Johns Hopkins University Press,
1996), 1:318.

35. *CW* 14: 326.

36. Philalethes, "The Secret of the Immortal Liquor called ALKAHEST," 22.

37. Cf. Demetrakopoulos, "Hestia, Goddess of the Hearth," 68.

insight possible, only dedication, fervid and pure. Alchemical psychology protects itself from salt by its composite thinking, in mixtures, a bit of this and a bit of that. Alchemical salt is always yielding its body to sulfur and mercury, to the love for it of spirit and soul, *fiat mihi*, let it be done to me, receptive to other powers, touching them and in touch with what it is not, the alien and unredeemed. For the function of salt is not its own conservation, but the preservation of whatever it touches. Images of the Virgin Mary, welcoming the alien, letting all things come to her and affording protection by giving her body to whatever their condition, by giving that touch which brings out their flavor and blesses their earth— this presents the soluble salt, Stella Maris. For as Arnold of Villanova said, "The salt that can be melted" is the desirable salt.[38] "Prepare this salt till it is rendered sweet."[39]

As a final example of the fervor of salt, or what the alchemist Khunrath[40] imagines as a hell fire in the midst of salt, perhaps a too-bright light in which purity burns with a consuming passion, we close with an "alchemical text" by D.H. Lawrence from his 1915 novel *The Rainbow*, the chapter called "First Love."[41]

The scene is set among haystacks under the moon, at a wedding feast. Images of fire and darkness pervade, and those familiar alchemical opposites appear when "red fire glinted on a white or silken skirt."
The principal figure, Ursula, "wanted to let go":

> She wanted to reach and be amongst the flashing stars, she wanted to race with her feet and be beyond the confines of this earth. She was mad to be gone. It was as if a hound were straining on the leash, ready to hurl itself after a nameless quarry into the dark.

She invites Skrebensky to dance. "It was his will and her will...locked in one motion, yet never fusing, never yielding one to the other."

---

38. *CW* 14: 240.

39. *The Glory of the World* (*HM* 1: 177).

40. *CW* 14: 337; *HM* 1: 176–77.

41. D.H. Lawrence, *The Rainbow* (London: Penguin Books, 1995), ch. 11. Other passages exhibiting saline, lunar, metallic metaphors, and even a chemical view of human character in the relationship of Ursula and Skrebensky, appear in ch. 15, "The Bitterness of Ecstasy."

> As the dance surged heavily on, Ursula was aware of some influence looking in upon her...Some powerful, glowing sight was looking right into her...She turned, and saw a great white moon...And her breast opened to it...She stood filled with the full moon, offering herself...She wanted the moon to fill in to her, she wanted more, more communion with the moon, consummation.

Skrebensky takes her hand and wraps a big dark cloak around her, and they sit. She desires desperately to fling off her clothing and flee away to the moon, "the clean free moonlight." Skrebensky, too, takes on a metallic quality, "a dark, impure magnetism. He was the dross, people were the dross."

> Skrebensky, like a load-stone weighed on her ...He was inert, and he weighed on her ...Oh, for the coolness and entire liberty and brightness of the moon. Oh, for the cold liberty to be herself...She felt like bright metal.

And her hands clench "in the dewy brilliance of the moon, as if she were mad." Then a strange rage fills her and her hands feel like metal blades of destruction. "Let me alone," she said. She throws off his dark cloak and walks towards the moon "silver-white herself."

They begin again to dance, and a struggle starts between them. She feels "a fierce, white, cold passion in her heart." And though he presses his body on her, as if to make her feel inert along with him, there remains in her body a "cold, indomitable passion." "She was cold and unmoved as a pillar of salt." To him she feels "cold and hard and compact of brilliance as the moon itself," and he wishes to set a bond around her and compel her to his will.

> They went towards...the great new stacks of corn...silver and present under the night-blue sky...the silvery-bluish air. All was intangible, a burning of cold, glimmering, whitish-steely fires. He was afraid of the great moon-conflagration of the corn-stacks...He knew he would die.

Ursula becomes aware of the power she holds: "A sudden lust seized her, to lay hold of him and tear him and make him into nothing." Her hands feel hard and strong as blades and her face gleams "bright and inspired." Skrebensky again draws her close to him.

> And timorously, his hands went over her, over the salt compact bril-
> liance of her body...If he could but net her brilliant, cold, salt-burn-
> ing body in the soft iron of his own hands...He strove...with all his
> energy to enclose her, to have her. And always she was burning and
> brilliant and hard as salt, and deadly.

He puts his mouth to her mouth, "though it was like putting his face into some awful death," and her kiss was "hard and fierce and burning corrosive as the moonlight..."

> Cold as the moon and burning as a fierce salt. Till gradually his soft
> iron yielded, yielded, and she was there fierce, corrosive, seething
> with his destruction, seething like some cruel, corrosive salt around
> the last substance of his being, destroying him, destroying him in the
> kiss. And her soul crystallized with triumph, and his soul was dis-
> solved with agony and annihilation.

I have let D.H. Lawrence present the figures and scene of my conclusion for several reasons. First, to exhibit again the connection between
psychology and literature, to suggest their interchangeability. Second, to
bring witness to the ever-presence of alchemical imagination—in this case
the *sol et luna* conjunction as sulfuric iron and salt. (I do not believe we can
reduce these images and this rhetoric to the influence upon Lawrence of
his father, a miner, or of the mining milieu of his native place.) Third, to
show personalities as composed of and carried by imaginal substances—
metallic seeds, chemicals, impersonal minerals, the hard and enduring
natures of the gods working through our wills. And, fourth, to raise a veil
and sound a warning concerning undifferentiated lunar consciousness.

As the twentieth century was setting, a full moon was rising. Much as
solar enlightenment and its obsession with clarity, optics, measurement,
royalty and categories of hierarchical order possessed the Western mind
from the sixteenth century until the Romantic revolution, so moonbeams
infiltrated into the late twentieth century: Right-sided brains and left-
handed cults; herbals and vegetables, fragrant candles and healing rites;
fears of seas rising and the aquifers going saline; wiccans, pop-visions of
Our Lady, Artemis freedoms, Diana power, lesbian politics, the ordina-
tion of women priests; women governors, senators, generals, CEOs, history as "herstory"; marching mothers and the salt tears of grieving, the

moon-balm of compassion to all creatures large and small. All the god-
desses crowded within. "The Feminine" as a fervor of salt; new sanity and
old lunacy indistinguishable in the moonlight.

Too close to the moon can be madness. "Love burns in changes of the
moon." Says Robert Duncan, "She comes so near to earth/And makes
men mad./O misery!" ("The Venice Poem"). We watch this moon too
close to earth in Ursula, whose lunacy is a death-dealing fanaticism, bitter, assertive, caustic, sterile, corrosive salt. We witness Ursula's body
turning to salt as she becomes infused with her subjectivity. Like Lot's
wife, she is self-occupied. Because salt is the soul of the body, it can reach
us through body-subjectivity. We become pure body-experience, and
transmute the event of the other into a mere instrument of the experience. Thus the body turns to salt; it remains untouched, its virginity preserved even while it is being embraced because no conjunction is happening, only the intense experience of subjectivity.

There is a confusion here between the urge for purity and the desire
for liberty. The Vestal Virgin submitted utterly; there was no possibility
of imagining liberty together with purity. The result of this confusion is
a fervid and lonely purism, a vestigial virgin without her ritual and iso-
lated from her cult, burning with divine eros, yet seeking the white light
for herself, her devotion to the moon poisoned by the salt of subjectivity. "People were the dross." Purism is the salt in the soul that allows no
recovery; it is also the passion for revenge. "Carthage must be exterminated," said obsessed, fanatical Cato; its soil sown with salt. Purism as
utter destruction.

Each planet, each worship, each archetypal perspective has its kind
of terror. There is a terror in the moon, in the purity of a single-minded
devotion that its salt can claim. The terror arises not simply from its so-
called dark side, from Lamia and Hecate's bitch or Lilith, but from the
moon's sway over the salt in the seas and our microcosmic flood. From
the analysis in this chapter we may understand purism as the fixation of
salt into a literalization of the preservative principle.

Owing to the inherent relation between Luna and Sal, purism is the
main danger in any devotion to the moon. To invoke the moon is to invite

the salt,[42] and unless we are trained in the nature and power of salt as were the alchemists and the Vestal Virgins, we become unwitting terrorists of the night, no matter how noble our dedication. Fanatical singleness frees one from the power of the other but at the expense of destroying the other's core existence. We may stand tall, but we stand alone, cold and barren as the moon.

Ursula had not been trained in alchemical psychology where we learn that the moon is not a stopping place. Both alchemy and astrology consider the moon a way station to the other planets,[43] just as the microcosmic moon, the human psyche, indicates various gods. The moon implies others; it is no sovereign solar king producing its all-important, self-sufficient light out of itself. It reflects light from beyond itself. For an alchemical psychology, devotion to the moon extends to what the moon reflects—a variety of other powers.

In everyday use salt is an emetic and a purgative. It can rid us of poisons. In the right dilution it is medicinal and hastens healing. Because it purifies, it was sprinkled on the sacred flour and sacrificial animals by the Roman vestals. That purity was apportioned precisely, ritually, uncontaminated by any other element. Especially, no water. The virgins were issued only the amount of water they would use each day and the water was held in an unsteady jar (the *futile*) so that none could be kept. Purity cannot allow dilution.

We each need a Vestal Virgin to guide our hand in apportioning our fervid dedication and the grains of inherent bitterness that accompany dedication and give it its zest. The very same salt that is honest wisdom, sincere truth, common sense, ironic wit and subjective feeling is also salt

---

42. One name for salt was "common moon" (*HM* 1: 177). The affinity of *sal* and *luna* was metallurgically witnessed in the process of gold-making: When salt is added to a gold/silver *compositum* and it is exposed to red-hot heat for a period, the salt "attacks" the silver, driving it into the walls of the crucible where it forms sliver chloride, letting the purified gold run free. This process compares with the "attack" of salt on leprotic lunar reflection, freeing the light of intelligence from hyper-subjectivity. (R. J. Forbes, *Metallurgy in Antiquity*, 2nd ed. [Leiden: Brill, 1971], 180.)

43. *CW* 14: 217–18. "Luna represents the six planet…She is multi-natured."

the destroyer. Dosage[44] is the art of the salt; a touch of the virgin, not too much. This dosage only our individual taste and common sense can prescribe. Only our salt can taste its own requirements.

---

44. It was Paracelsus and his school (Debus, *The English Paracelsians*, 32–35) that "went to great pains to determine the correct dosage with their medicines." The concern with dosage derived most probably from the iatrochemistry of mineral and metallic salts as specific medicines. If the Paracelsians taught the art of dosing salts, salt was the principle that taught the Paracelsians.

Made in the USA
Middletown, DE
12 September 2024

60794828R00094